LEAVE
NO MAN
BEHIND

LEAVE NO MAN BEHIND

The Untold Story of the Rangers'
Unrelenting Search for
Marcus Luttrell, the Navy SEAL
Lone Survivor in Afghanistan

DR. TONY BROOKS
WITH BOB WELCH

DIVERSION
BOOKS

For more information, email info@diversionbooks.com

The views expressed in this publication are those of the author and do not necessarily reflect the official policy or position of the Department of Defense or the U.S. government.

The public release clearance of this publication by the Department of Defense does not imply Department of Defense endorsement or factual accuracy of the material.

Diversion Books
A division of Diversion Publishing Corp
www.diversionbooks.com

First Diversion Books edition, August 2021
First Diversion Paperback, January 2023
Hardcover ISBN: 9781635767353
Paperback ISBN: 9781635767797
eBook ISBN: 9781635767360

Printed in The United States of America

1 3 5 7 9 10 8 6 4 2

Library of Congress cataloging-in-publication data is available on file.

Cover photo courtesy of Oleg Zabielin/Alamy
Author photo by Jackie Phairow Photography
Jacket design by Tom Lau

First and foremost, to my wife, Heidi, I love you and couldn't do any of this alone. You are truly my guiding light. To my children, Ryle and Evynn: I hope my story encourages you to work as a team. As a team, even the toughest of objectives can be conquered. It is you that can bring others together to reach any goal. It is you who can accomplish anything with enough resolve, strategy, and teamwork. I look forward to seeing how you will change the world someday soon. I love all three of you with every ounce of my soul—and don't you ever forget it.

And to the men and women who have served: You are the heartbeat of America. You are the glue that keeps us together. May you never feel left behind.

CONTENTS

CONTENTS

AUTHOR'S NOTE

IN 2003, THE SAME YEAR I ENLISTED TO BECOME A US
Army Ranger, the movie *Return of the King* was released. In
director Peter Jackson's last film adaptation of J.R.R. Tolk-
ien's *Lord of the Rings* trilogy, its ending explains, in part, why
I wrote this book. In one of the final scenes, four of the Hobbits have returned from battle to their homeland, the "Shire."
Returned, you could say, from helping save the world, in this
case "Middle-earth."

They gather at a pub—not that any of the crowd there
notices. Amid a festive atmosphere, the attention of the other
patrons is focused on a giant pumpkin that someone has placed
at a nearby table. People are fascinated by it. But nobody pays
any attention to the home-from-war soldiers.

The viewer, of course, sees the irony. The viewer knows the
context: where the four young men have been. What they have
accomplished. And how the foursome—Frodo, Sam, Pippin, and
Merry—had left as boys and returned as men. They had gone to
war, risked it all, cheated death—all for the good of the Shire.
For their fellow citizens. For people just like the folks mesmer-
ized by the giant pumpkin.

Given the lack of attention paid them, they might as well
have been ghosts. Not a word is spoken in the scene, but the
eyes and subtle gestures of the four say it all. Initially, there's a
slight sense that they feel forgotten. But instead of slinking into

self-pity they exude something else: a subtle sense of pride. *They* know where they've been and what they've done—and, at the end of the day, that's all that really matters. They smile. Toast each other. It's time, the unspoken words suggest, to move on with their lives.

To that end, Sam catches the eyes of the bartender he was smitten with before he'd left for war—and he heads toward her like a heat-seeking missile. Ultimately, he marries her.

I CAN RELATE TO IT ALL, INCLUDING SAM'S ATTRACTION to a cute bartender, which pretty much mirrors my time before and after my deployments to Afghanistan and Iraq. And I can definitely relate to the "ghost" feeling. Nobody goes to war expecting a gala sendoff or comes home expecting to be waving to the crowd from a convertible in a ticker-tape parade. But soldiers who've served in Iraq and Afghanistan are, indeed, invisible. Few civilians notice them leave, notice they're gone, or notice them when they've returned.

What's more, beyond family and friends, few notice the ones who *don't* return—who give their lives for their country. What's lost in all this? Stories. Perspective. Understanding. The gap between soldier and civilian grows wider. And, given that we're all citizens of the same country, I find that an unnecessary shame.

I'm a people person; as a chiropractor, I deal with patients every day. If I had to work in a cubicle, cut off from people, I'd go nuts. I enjoy engaging other human beings. At age thirty-five, I was elected president of my local Rotary club in Washington state. I serve on a police foundation board. When I meet someone, I want to know what their story is—what they do for a living, where they're from, why they live where they live. The works.

But I noticed something when I returned from Afghanistan and Iraq: nobody seemed interested in hearing my story. Don't get me wrong. I don't consider myself any sort of hero. I didn't engage in that much combat. But like the foursome in the pub, I went to war. I put my life on the line for freedom. For the patrons of the pub, as it were.

Most civilians have so little interaction with, and understanding of, today's military, that they see someone's experience in Afghanistan and Iraq in one of two ways: in terms of political fodder, or in terms of stereotypical fodder. The former denigrates military personnel to pawns of presidents and political leaders, tainting them as extensions of the war-is-evil viewpoint. The latter suggests every soldier was an ace sniper, eluded capture by hundreds of marauders, and fired a machine gun day in and day out.

Neither is true. In terms of politics, hating war shouldn't mean hating—or disrespecting—the warrior. And in terms of stereotypes, the military is so much deeper and broader than combat heroes. I'm hardly the Global War on Terror's (GWOT) answer to Rambo; in fact, the only two people I've ever been compared to in cinematic terms are Forrest Gump, the earnest do-gooder played by Tom Hanks, and Peter Parker, Spider-Man's weaker side. But here's the thing: most soldiers who've served in Iraq or Afghanistan are probably far more like me than Rambo. We are ordinary men and women who have had the privilege of serving with extraordinary soldiers. And yet we, too, have stories worth telling—not for our collective egos, but for the collective education of our country.

So, consider this a different type of war story, with less emphasis on blood and guts than on honor, courage, and reality. I don't want to shout my story from the rooftop for some sort of self-edification. But, yeah, I do want my children to understand the amazing experience and heartache that their father endured. And I do want to help readers get beyond the military stereotypes that so often stifle civilians and soldiers from better understanding each other. I want them to experience a war story that has the grit and grist of war, complete with, unfortunately, unprecedented death on the American side, but may not include combat on a blockbuster-film scale.

To that end, I'm tempted to see this as Every Soldier's Afghanistan Story, but that would be naïve. You've heard it said, "Every child has different parents," the inference, of course, being that each kid's experience is uniquely different from the other siblings. In the same way, every soldier has a different war. This is just one Army Ranger's war. Nothing more. Nothing less.

It's just one small way of buying a beer for the folks enthralled with the pumpkin and saying: *Tell me about yourself. And then let me tell you about me—where I've been, what I've seen, and why it should matter to all of us who gather in this common place.*

In part, it's about soldiers preparing for, and going to, war. But its deeper essence is about coming home. For the soldiers and sailors who gave their lives for the cause of freedom—nineteen in my case, all of whom died together in nearly the same instant. And for the men who survived but, back home, too often feel as if they've been left behind.

Tony Brooks
Everett, Washington
June 2020

PROLOGUE

BIRD DOWN ON SAWTALO SAR

The Situation Report (SITREP): 36 hours since the crash of *Turbine 33*
1500 meters SSW of crash site

THE GLOW. I'LL NEVER FORGET THE GLOW. I SAW IT ON
the early morning of June 30, 2005, while those of us in the
75th Ranger Regiment scrambled up the side of Afghanistan's
9,364-foot Sawtalo Sar: a glow that, at first glance, looked as
beautiful and benign as the flame on a candle—the candle I
imagined on the restaurant table between me and Heidi, the
beautiful bartender in Seattle I hoped to ask out when I got
home. *If* I got home.

As we got closer, however, the glow took on a sinister
appearance—looking less like a candle than a funeral pyre.
And, really, what else should I have expected? We were closing in
on the charred remains of one of our MH-47 helicopters. Some
pro-Taliban national—probably one of Ahmad Shah's boys—
had gotten lucky while firing a rocket-propelled grenade from

an RPG-7. For the sixteen men aboard—eight Navy SEALs and eight Army Special Operations aviators—the chance of survival was obviously slim. But my positive nature wouldn't let me give up hope. If even one man was still alive, it would salvage at least a smidgeon of success. But, one way or the other, all sixteen were coming home. That's why "the Regiment" was here. To make sure no man was left behind.

The 75th Ranger Regiment is an elite airborne light infantry combat unit within the US Army. And from the moment I began training in Ft. Benning, Georgia, with hopes of being part of that elite group, it had been hammered into us with all the subtlety of a nail-gun. *Every damn soldier comes home. Period.* Now it was time to fulfill the promise we'd each made to ourselves, our unit, our country.

The terrain was steep, not unlike the Sierra Nevada mountains just east of where I'd grown up in Roseville, California. The load on my body was heavy—armor alone runs thirty pounds with magazines and I had some sixty to eighty pounds of total gear—but the load on my mind still heavier. We had a job to do, yeah, but that didn't mean checking our humanity at the door; these were our brothers we'd come to get. Guys who, like me, might have had a fleeting thought of home just as the rocket-propelled grenade had torched their helicopter in mid-air.

Now, nearly two miles above sea level, we made our way closer to the wreckage: tail number 146, Evil Empire, call sign *Turbine 33*. Shot out of the sky by an anti-coalition fighter the day before. If the first sight of the charred and smoldering helicopter had weakened my gut, the smell nearly brought me to my knees—and we weren't even at the site yet. It was like nothing I'd ever experienced, a stinging, pungent odor that made it hard to breathe. Burned flesh.

"Take a knee," a team leader barked.

PROLOGUE

We rested for a moment. I drank some water and realized I was already running low. I wanted to down every last drop—just to clean out the stench—but sunrise, I knew, would bring relentless heat, and I'd need every ounce. I spit, as if I could rid myself of the rancid odor.

Welcome, I quietly said to myself, to the shit sandwich called war.

At age twenty-two, this was not what I thought it was going to be on my first mission as a Ranger. This wasn't the gallant-fighting stuff of Pat Tillman, the soldier—and former NFL football player—who'd inspired me to enlist after 9/11. This wasn't the stuff of *Black Hawk Down*. Where was the anticipation of battle? Where was Good snuffing out Evil?

I was here to fight. We all were. But that didn't make us murderers. We simply wanted to do what we could to protect our country, and if that involved killing, so be it. This mission was necessary, but it didn't feel good. It didn't feel liberating, as I thought my time here would feel. I was here to avenge an attack on my country. Now I was faced with trying to find what remained of sixteen men blown up in a helicopter. I had no idea what we were going to find—or *weren't* going to find. But whatever it was, it wasn't the vanquish-the-enemy stuff I'd expected.

We moved forward into the dark swath of tall timber—mainly pine, daylight would show. With my M4 Carbine in hand and under the press of our gear, we moved on. Hour after hour. We scampered up slopes, jumped down boulders, slipped, sweated, swore, and bled, the latter courtesy of the inevitable falls in the dark. Headlamps would have put glow-in-the-dark targets on our backs for the Taliban; instead, we made our way using night-vision monoculars, which helped but made the world a fuzzy blur of green, as if we were swimming in algae-thick waters.

Keep going. Keep moving. Don't stop till we get to the crash site.

The sixteen men had been blown out of the sky while preparing to do just what we were doing—coming to help their brothers: four Navy SEALs who'd been dropped on Sawtalo Sar under cover of darkness to find and monitor Ahmad Shah, a notorious Taliban-friendly leader, and his small group of men. The four Americans had been ambushed after they'd been spotted by Afghan goat herders who had obviously reported their findings to the Taliban—although there's thought that, even without the goat herders, the Taliban-friendly militia, which knew every crevice and tree on the mountain, knew the "infidels" were prowling in its backyard. At any rate, the US mission had been compromised. Though I didn't know it at the time, only one of the four men, Marcus Luttrell, had survived, his story told in the book (2007) and movie (2013) *Lone Survivor.*

Now we'd arrived to rescue—or recover—the sixteen who'd come to help the four-man recon team. We'd heard that the crew of an accompanying helicopter had witnessed the crash and fireball that followed. A few A-10 "Sandy" flights had flown low over the burning remnants of the helicopter shortly afterward. Their report? No survivors. They saw only the terrible, white-hot flames and roiling black smoke billowing into the sky above the mountain on which we now walked. And yet how could you not hope that some had managed to survive?

Dead or alive, these sixteen weren't just anybody. They were sons, husbands, fathers, boyfriends, fiancés, friends. *Americans.* And, whatever shape we found them in, we needed to take care of them.

A radio squawked.

"PJs are there," my team leader soon reported to us. Air Force Special Warfare, Pararescue men—called PJs—are highly trained to rescue, recover, and medically treat downed military personnel and their aircraft. I was glad they'd arrived on the site—and anxious to hear what they'd found.

As dawn approached, I got my first real look at Afghanistan from the side of the mountain. Many think of Afghanistan as a large, lifeless desert. It's not. On the mountainside, we walked under towering pines and through carpets of dense ferns. Wisps of low clouds and fog grazed the mountains around us, remnants of thunderstorms that had unleashed torrents from the sky above just hours earlier. It was beautiful, unlike anything I'd ever seen. It was hard to comprehend that we were walking on a battlefield, one where an enemy—or the carnage that enemy had created—lay just ahead, just out of sight.

I was facing to the east as the sun slowly crept into view and warmed the valley below us. After a few minutes of staring at this lifeless valley, I flipped up my night-vision monocular. Day had arrived on the slopes of Sawtalo Sar. The safety blanket of darkness was gone; our enemy now had a much better chance of spotting us. The element of surprise died with the light. Worst, at least for us: they knew this country almost as well as the goat herders. In short, we were playing a road game, and everyone knows how hard it is to win on the road.

My mind ramped to "full alert"; the light was perfect for an ambush. My trigger-finger rested on the cold steel of my M4. As I scanned the mountains, I saw signs of human activity, trails, in the clear-cut areas that had been logged. Still, it felt as if we were sitting ducks—even if we did have more firepower than a lot of small nations.

Buzzzzzzz. You could hear a slight humming sound coming from above, which was always a welcome sound for me. Not a bee, not a hummingbird, but distant helicopters, drones, and planes. The sound reminded me that every air asset available was up there somewhere, ready to warn us of any enemy movement, and ready to strike on our behalf. Beyond my buddies in the 75th, that sound generated the only feeling of comfort I knew, the only assurance that I was connected to something beyond our unit.

We were awaiting word from the PJs about what they'd found, and about what medical supplies and personnel would be needed to save whatever men, if any, might have survived. I could barely swallow, the nervous energy translating to my mouth; it felt as if I'd been chewing on a cotton ball. I grabbed my camelback straw and took a small sip, just enough to wet my mouth, again trying to conserve as much of my water as possible.

"Whataya think, Brooks?" whispered Todd, my teammate, and the senior private in my squad. "Could any of 'em still be alive?"

"Hoping. Think there's a chance."

That's just me: the eternal optimist. The kid who could come into the living room on Christmas morning, find a pile of horse crap and say, "Where's the pony?!!!" The kid who, despite a doctor's warning that I would never qualify for military service after I'd blown out a knee, became an Army Ranger. The kid who, gone off to war for a couple of years, still thought he had a chance with the fiery bartender from Cowgirls Inc. back in Seattle.

Now, in the Afghan morning, my skin was damp, my hair on end, my nerves frayed. Suddenly, something moved, back in the trees. I readied my rifle. Out walked two of our own, heading slowly toward my unit. PJs. And it was clear they had news. We gathered like moths to a flame, as if not only anxious to hear the news, but, at the same time, fearing it.

1

OUT OF THE WHEELHOUSE

THOUGH I TEND TO BE ANALYTICAL—THAT'S A EUPHEMISTIC term for "nerd"—the moment I decided to join the military came as impulsively as a retaliatory punch. I was eighteen, a freshman at the University of Arizona. At the time, I rarely watched television, but for some reason I had switched on the TV that morning, September 11, 2001. I was stunned by the footage of the first of the two Twin Towers collapsing, but it was an image within that image that gripped me deepest: the tiny speck of a human being plummeting fifty-plus stories to his or her death.

I knew instantly that the crash into the tower had not been an accident, but a "holy-shit" act of terrorism. And I needed to respond. Seeing the first plane ram the building jolted my emotional equilibrium. Watching the smoke roil skyward sickened my stomach. But knowing that this person had either fallen from the building or chosen to jump triggered an anger-fueled call to action on my part.

I would, I decided then and there, enlist in the military. Fight. Tell this enemy, with bullets and bombs instead of words, to never try something like this again. *Ever.*

After further review, I suppose some analyzing came into play, but it was lightning fast. Instinctual. Personal. *You attack us, I'm attacking you.* It was as if, in that moment, I decided if that life had been snuffed by some ruthless terrorist, then whatever speck of life I represented was willing to fight so nobody else would have to die such a humiliating, tragic, unnecessary death.

Not that anybody who knew me would have expected such a response from me, myself included. It was nothing short of a sea change in who I was, and who I would become, as a human being. To appreciate how out-of-the-blue the idea of military enlistment was for me, understand that:

A. After finishing in the top ten percent of my class at Oakmont High in Roseville, I was studying business at a major university and enjoying the fraternity party scene—in other words, deeply ensconced in a world as far from the military as you could get, a world whose endgame was pleasure and success, not pain and sacrifice;

B. my father was president of the family oil company. I had the means to get a good education and make a very good living. As my interest in getting a degree in business waned, I was considering becoming a geologist, or even a doctor;

C. though my grandfathers both served in the Korean
    War, I wasn't, as they say, from a "military family."
    Though the Brookses loved America, we were not an
    overly flag-waving family;

D. at 5'9" tall and 165 lbs., I did not exactly fit the
    Sergeant Rock stereotype;

E. I had no particular interest in, or experience with,
    weapons.

Hell, I was a golfer; if I was at a range, it wasn't for target
practice but for honing my swing. I'd grown up living the American
Dream. In summers, when I was a young teenager, Mom
would drop me off at Sierra View Country Club, where our family
belonged, and I would play golf all day, stopping only to scarf
down burgers, Cokes, and shakes conveniently placed on my
father's tab. People like that don't take up arms. They take up
bocce ball. They slap down credit cards. They order in extravagant
pizza. But, no, they don't enlist in the military.

"Dad," I said to my father, Steve, in fall 2001, "I'm not sure
college is working out so well."

There was a pause on the other end of the line.

"What's going on? Is everything okay?"

I sniffled, trying to gather my composure—trying to not
mention my sub-2.0 GPA, a freefall caused by too much partying
and too little sense of purpose. For the first time in my life, I
was failing miserably—and the answer, for once, didn't seem to
be to "work harder." The answer seemed to be to try something
totally different.

"I just don't like what I am doing here," I said. "It feels *wrong*.
It feels like I should be doing something else. Something more
meaningful."

3

I could almost feel the disappointment from my father, but he said nothing.

"I think I want to join the military."

I could almost hear the gulp on the other end of the call.

"Anthony, finish the year and we can talk about it. You can't make a decision this important so quickly. This college experience is a moment in time. You have a lot of life to do something more meaningful."

Even though it wasn't exactly what I wanted to hear, I knew he was right.

"You're right. I need to think about this some more."

MY SUDDEN INTEREST IN THE MILITARY WAS SO OUT OF the wheelhouse that when I told my mother, Kathy, about wanting to be a Ranger, she was thinking the US Forest Service. Yogi Bear. Seriously. A park ranger. Checking hiking permits. Telling stories around campfires in the evening. That sort of thing.

Once she understood what I was really talking about, she and my father weren't opposed to the idea, but neither were they jumping up in mid-air, clicking their heels. They advised me to get more schooling under my belt, code speak, I imagined, for "put the idea on the backburner and you'll soon forget you even had it on the stove." Deep down, I wonder if they didn't figure that the war on terror would be over by the time I was ready to join; surely I would come to my senses and return to college.

I did as they suggested, shifting my major from business to geology in the process, but that didn't give me any more study traction—or peace of mind—than I had before. I was still lost in some Bermuda Triangle of purposelessness. When Pat Tillman enlisted to become an Army Ranger in May 2002, I only redoubled my commitment to do the same.

As instinctively as seeing that tiny human fall on 9/11 made me want to join the military, hearing about Tillman made me want to follow in his footsteps. True, as an ASU Sun Devil he had attended the rival school of my Arizona Wildcats, but I loved the guy's guts, grit, and conscience. Here was one of the finest players in the NFL, a guy who'd just been offered $3.6 million over the next three years to play for the Cardinals. And yet he turned his back on such wealth to serve his punched-in-the-gut country.

That was me. I don't say this with any chest-beating bravado, but despite my life of middle-class privilege, my parents had instilled in me a sense of integrity and conscience. Life was about doing the right thing. And even if none of my other friends had been similarly inspired, this was the right thing to do.

But it was a huge risk, and risk-taking had not been part of my childhood repertoire. Remember, I was an analyzer, not an impulsive adventurer. If I was with my buddies and someone wanted to risk some sort of juvenile escapade, I would only participate if I "ran the numbers" and it added up. So, my sudden shift toward going off to war represented a clear departure in my calculate-and-proceed-with-caution demeanor.

That first year in college, the only noble thing I remember doing was standing up for a friend who was about to be hazed unmercifully as a pledge in the same fraternity to which I belonged. I didn't care for hazing, period. Plus, I knew my buddy had an early-morning ROTC event and couldn't afford to show up drunk as a skunk. I intervened—and though it didn't win me any friends with my frat brothers, I saved my buddy's butt. Ironically, I was named the vice president shortly after being initiated.

I'd been raised with a strong sense of integrity; the worst thing we could ever do, my father said, was lie. Back in the days when boys and girls delivered newspapers, I had a route. At times, I would need a substitute, younger kids who were enthusiastic to help. But I don't think I ever paid them. And that memory has stuck with me. It bothers me that I hadn't displayed more integrity.

Years later, my mother and I, in separate interviews with a journalist, were asked what movie character best described who I was. With little hesitation—and with no knowledge of each other's answer—we both answered "Forrest Gump." I said it because of a sense of nerdiness I saw in myself. Though most of my friends were jocks during my middle school and high school years, I was only a superstar with the leading edge of "techies." I became Cisco Network-certified at age fifteen.

But my mother, Kathy, saw my "Gumption" as something else: *earnestness* ("sincere and intense conviction"). That might be an understatement. I'd stood up to bullies who were badgering a friend—even though my mother reminds me that I was bullied a bit myself, in part because of my asthma, in part because I was built like a ski pole with two wings as ears. And when I made a wrong choice—say, not paying the substitutes who helped me on my paper route—I felt genuine remorse. Mom's Gump comparison, she said, was also because of my asthma; she saw that as my equivalent of Forrest's "crooked-like-a-question-mark" back that forced him to wear leg braces.

Though I had been raised in a cocoon of comfort, I shared Pat Tillman's sense that bigger things were at play than money and materialism. I tried to eke out another year of college, but my new-found passion to join the military won out. In January 2003 I quit school and, a few months later, after the war in Iraq had kicked off, enlisted. By now, my folks could see which way the wind was blowing for me—toward Afghanistan, and possibly Iraq—and they didn't even try to stop me.

I enlisted.

It wasn't out of a sense of apologetics for my entitlement, a way to prove I was as hungry and down-to-earth as the next guy. It was out of a sense of duty to my country. It's simply what I knew I needed to do: Not just become a soldier. But become part of the elite 75th Ranger Regiment, among the finest fighting units of the world.

Weird, I know, but I'd always liked rules and the military was full of them. What's more, my father was a fairly competitive guy, particularly in the business world. Some of that had rubbed off on me. I liked the challenge of proving myself at the highest level—if to nobody else than to the guy who stared back at me in the mirror each night.

I was never an elite athlete. I was never the smartest kid in the class, graduating high school with a 3.7 GPA. But I was just enough of an overachiever to have the chutzpah to believe in myself, and just enough of an underdog to have a chip on my shoulder. What's more, I had that Gump-esque blindness to those around me, as if I lived in a world all my own. Some might translate that to "he didn't know what he didn't know." And, frankly, that's probably true.

Even my mother would tell you I was a late bloomer; I was "born old," as they say, on November 29, 1982. A dreamer. A big-picture kid. Driven to succeed.

Michael Jackson's groundbreaking album *Thriller* and the movie *E.T.* were released the month I was born. The third space shuttle launched. The Vietnam Veterans Memorial was dedicated. *Late Night with David Letterman* had debuted earlier in the year. *Dynasty* and *Hill Street Blues* were among the hot TV shows. For the United States, it was a relatively peaceful time, although 700,000 demonstrators gathered in New York City's Central Park protesting the proliferation of nuclear weapons. Economically,

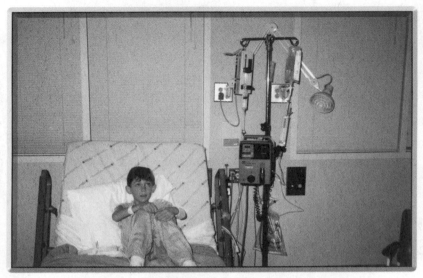

Hospital stay with "breathing issues." Not exactly Ranger material if you ask me.

a severe recession descended like a rancid fog, as if my birth had triggered it.

At age five, then again at age nine, I was hospitalized because of extreme breathing issues. The second time, I was blue when I arrived at the ER. Whenever that happened, I felt as if someone were standing on my chest. I hated that I had this weakness and I would do anything I could to hide it from those around me. It was a hard deficiency to hide, but I found a way, and I was pretty good at it. I was the kid who was never particularly gifted physically, but always found a way to "go to the head of the class."

I wouldn't call myself a teacher's pet, but I connected well with most instructors because I took learning seriously, listened intently, and always wanted to be the best student in the class. Here's what I learned: the harder you work, the easier it will be on the teacher and, so, the more they'll like you for that very reason.

Often, in my math classes, I'd find myself teaching the students around me who were struggling. It wasn't that I was more intelligent, but I thrived in a didactic model. If a teacher told me something, *boom*, it was locked into my memory as if placed in a safe-deposit box. Around me, classmates would be madly scrawling on their pads. I rarely took notes. As long as I heard it from a teacher's mouth, I would remember it. It only enhanced my learning to see something on a white board—if there was any hint of ambiguity, seeing a problem solved made it crystal-clear in my mind.

I first discovered my ability to visualize math problems in my head when I was in second grade. At that time, I was put in an experimental class that consisted of half second-graders and half third-graders. After testing, I was quickly identified as an advanced-class kid for math. But lest this start sounding like a "brag," let me point out that while I was ahead of my class academically, it was a different story in other areas. Physically and emotionally, I was like the kid who missed his school bus and is running down the street yelling, "Hey, wait for me, wait for me!"

I was short, skinny, dorky. Never a bully, but sometimes *bullied*. I think I was in two fights my entire life, one of them because I was defending a friend who was getting picked on.

I was blessed with a loving little sister, Kristina, and I was close with my little brother, Michael, two years my junior. We played a lot—and competed a lot—as kids. I was Hulk Hogan; he was Macho Man Randy Savage. I was Mario, he was Luigi. We would often get dressed up in karate gis and go "toe to toe" in our living room for fun. He was something of a history and military nut, and grew up as a rabid fan of US Army Rangers.

"Someday," he was forever reminding me, "I'm gonna be an Army Ranger." So, if there was a latent seed that had been planted about being part of this, I suppose I owe it to him. It's

This is evidence of my martial arts superiority over my brother Michael during one of our "combat sessions."

almost as if the idea was always there, in the back of my mind, but I needed something to germinate it. The attack on America was that something. Give an assist to *Black Hawk Down,* a movie that was released in January 2002, four months after 9/11. It was about a Ranger mission in Somalia that turned to disaster. But that didn't deter me, it inspired me. Those warriors, Rangers, fought their way out of the lion's den. My heart swelled with pride as I watched them fighting and running the "Mogadishu Mile" to safety.

I checked out the Army, Navy, and Marines. Not being much a fan of water, I crossed the Navy off my list and sat down with the Marines. They also had a thing for water. No thanks.

"What is it that you really want to do or be?" the Army recruiter asked me.

His question forced me to really decide. And I did.

"I want to be an Airborne Ranger," I said.

"You sure about that?"

I nodded yes. The Army recruiter looked at my slight build and, I imagine, paired that with a home address that placed me in among Roseville's tonier sections. I caught a look of doubt in his eyes and his grasping-for-straws next statement.

"You realize that your ASVAB (Armed Services Vocational Aptitude Battery) scores qualify you for any job—right?" I caught his drift: I was smart enough to be handed a cushy desk job. It's what he didn't say, but I suspected he believed, that inspired me: he doubted I could cut it with an elite combat unit.

Perfect; just what I needed. My passion to succeed was only fueled by those who dared to doubt me. When filling out enlistment papers in December 2003, I insisted on taking the "Option 40" route, a program that guaranteed I would get to attend Airborne training and the Ranger Indoctrination Program (RIP) immediately following. And at the very least, I was going to *attempt* to become a Ranger.

So, yeah, between 9/11 and the doubters, when I left to serve my country in early 2004, I did so not only with a passion for revenge, but with at least a slight chip on my shoulder. The attack pissed me off, plain and simple. And the military, I figured, was my chance to even the score, vent my anger, and— even if I didn't realize it at the time—test who I was as a human being.

2

READILY WILL I DISPLAY
THE INTESTINAL FORTITUDE

SITREP: August 2004, 10 months before the crash of
Turbine 33
Inside the Ranger Indoctrination Program

STAFF SERGEANT FADER HAD ONE OF THOSE
linebacker-coach voices that suggested the guy smoked a pack
of cigarettes every day—before lunch. At Fort Benning, Georgia,
in the late summer of 2004, Fader's job description must have
read: "Make life hell for recruits. Act like an asshole. Weed out
the wannabes. Create cold-blooded killers. Repeat."

It didn't take much for this brick house of a Ranger to invoke
fear in the most fear-adverse of men. Chuck Norris would have
wet his pants at the sight of this dude. And I wept for the insurgents in Iraq or Afghanistan who dared to stand in Fader's way.

"I am gonna punish you all—until someone quits!" he yelled
during our first-night drills. "And I don't care how long it takes.
I am here all night. Do all of your buddies a favor: *Quit!*"

I absolutely loved the guy. Just one more reason *not* to quit. One more reason to keep going, to prove that the country-club kid could handle an M4 Carbine and a fast-rope down from a helicopter in total darkness as well as the next guy. One more reason to prove wrong the doctor who said my ripped-up knee would prevent me from ever being in the military.

I had been a pretty decent basketball player—I made a competitive non-school team when I was twelve and drew the nickname "Silk" because of the smoothness of my shot. Then it happened in the spring of 1999. I was a high school sophomore, playing in a pickup basketball game at the park with my best friend, Blair. We had won our third game in a row when I stole a pass and headed for an easy layup, feeling particularly cool in my Michael Jordan gear. I gathered myself for the leap to the hoop for the easy basket.

"Behind you!" Blair yelled.

Glancing back, I realized an opponent was already airborne, hoping to swat my shot halfway to San Francisco. *Nope. Not gonna happen. Not today.* Ramping to maximum speed, I drove hard off my left leg and reached high for a right-handed layup, watched the ball spin obediently off the backboard and descend toward the hoop. *In your face, Dude.*

I was doomed the minute my right leg touched down. *Snap.* My knee exploded in excruciating pain.

"Oh, shiiiiit!" I yelled, writhing in pain. "Son of a bitch! Awwwwwwwwww!"

It was as if someone was carving out my knee with a sharp knife. I was livid. I hated to fail. And I knew the injury was bad. And getting worse. It went from knife-carving pain to throbbing to burning.

"What's wrong?" said Blair, rushing to my side. "Your ankle?"

I screamed more obscenities. I was inconsolable. I grabbed my right leg at the knee, wriggling around like a lizard in a frying pan.

Later, at the office of an orthopedic surgeon—himself a military veteran—I learned that my right anterior cruciate ligament, my medial collateral ligament, and parts of my medial and lateral meniscus were all torn. It was a trifecta of disaster. I remember three things about the orthopedic surgeon incident that, years later when I'd shown up at the Ranger Indoctrination Program in Georgia, helped define me as a human being.

First, I remember the surgeon breaking the news to me with what seemed like slow-motion words. "Sorry . . . son . . . but . . . you . . . are . . . done . . . with . . . sports."

My eyes turned glassy. *What? How am I going to—? This can't be happening.*

"I'm sorry," he said, talking as much to my parents as to me, "but only a few elite athletes recover from an injury with the severity of this one. Frankly, I've never seen one worse in a teenager."

Then he looked me right in the eyes. "Oh, and I don't know if you have any interest in military service, but I'm sorry. You can forget about that, too."

So that was Thing Two, a loss that, at least at the time, made me feel like the restaurant chef in that scene from *Dumb and Dumber*—released when I was twelve—when Lloyd (played by Jim Carrey) rips the guy's heart out, places it in a to-go bag, and hands it to him. Not because I had any thought of serving in the military, but for the simple fact that I had to eliminate something from possibility. Being the dreamer I was, I never wanted a door to close on me. Any door. Everything, I figured, was possible with enough grit, determination, and strategy.

The third and last thought that would define me came just before I fell asleep the first night after the injury—and was accompanied by the slightest of smiles. The layup I'd attempted just before blowing out my knee? I'd made that baby!

MY BASIC TRAINING/INFANTRY SCHOOL EXPERIENCE

was emotionally jarring. One minute you're living a life of luxury, freedom, and individualism back home, the next minute assimilating to a life of deprivation, subordination, and conformity. Physically, however, it hadn't been that tough. I don't say that to brag; it was simply the truth.

Back then, the many steps to becoming a US Army Airborne Ranger started with OSUT (One Station Unit Training), which combined BCT (Basic Combat Training) and AIT (Advanced Individual Training—or, generically, Infantry School). After Infantry School, it would be Airborne School, then the feared Ranger Indoctrination Program (RIP). After that, you could call yourself a Ranger and could dawn the coveted "tan beret."

However, even that came with conditions. You would then have to earn a spot at US Army Ranger School, which would usually take about a year of training and combat as a Ranger. After earning your spot and passing Ranger School, you were then eligible to be in a leadership position, and frankly, allowed to stay in the 75th Ranger Regiment. If you didn't earn the Ranger tab, which was the reward for passing Ranger School, you would not be welcomed back to the 75th Ranger Regiment and would be sent on your way to an infantry unit of the Army's choosing.

After my first fourteen weeks, I finished Basic and Infantry School. My folks flew to Georgia for the graduation ceremony. I'd just spent the last three-plus months being hammered into a soldier. And I was the son of a man—a great man, by the way—who never wore his emotions on his sleeve. But there I was, getting all choked up right there in front of my folks, Steve and Kathy. If you grow up in a home without much love and then leave, there's no looking back; and there's nobody coming to your graduation. I wasn't emotional because I'd survived basic training; I was emotional because, for the first time in my life, I realized what amazing parents I had. And, quietly, I grieved for buddies who had nobody in the audience there to support them.

It was the first juxtaposition of the civilian/military divide that I would wrestle with—and appreciate—for the rest of my life, this idea that the Army could mold you into a soldier but could never deprive you of your humanity. Unless, of course, you let it.

As a soldier, you are to hide any perceived weakness so it can't be used against you or your brothers in arms. This attitude is amplified in the Special Operations community where men would rather die than be relieved from their unit for a perceived weakness. As a member of Special Operations, you are volunteering for the position, and can quit at any moment. You can also be relieved for sucking at what you do. I wanted neither to be the case for me. That said, I didn't want to come out of the meat-grinder a few years later as one of two things:

    A. A deranged, unfeeling, insensitive lout;
    B. Dead.

AFTER BASIC TRAINING AND INFANTRY SCHOOL, I headed down the road at Fort Benning to United States Army Airborne School. It was a virtual vacation compared to what was to come. Much of it was just the basics of landing safely out of an airplane or helicopter. How to fall. What gear to wear. Stuff like that. We were only required to do five jumps from a C130. And, for the first time, we had weekends off.

We maximized that time—in a Ranger way. Three of my new-found buddies—Eric Delong, Felipe Peters, and Sam Crino—and I would drink our way through the watering holes in Columbus, Georgia, as if competing in an Olympic decathlon. Only the different events weren't the stuff of sprints, hurdles, and jumps, but Coors Light, Bud Light, and a few shots of whiskey and Jägermeister. This is where a bond of brotherhood formed that continues to this day. I could call any one of these guys and, despite being separated by more than a decade—despite living in different corners of the country, despite each of us taking distinctly different life paths—we would not skip a beat to help each other out.

We were dumb enough to *not* know "when to say when," but smart enough to walk, rather than drive, to our motel when the tenth and final event—"bar closing"—was over.

Felipe, aka Felipe "Petie" Peters, was among my favorites. He was Texas and Arkansas-raised, Mexican-born, and German-descended, a redneck combination of *King of the Hill*'s Boomhauer, Jeff Foxworthy, and Bill Clinton. I compare him to the former president—a comparison he probably wouldn't enjoy—because they both have this ability to make everyone in a room think they are the greatest thing since the "like" button on Facebook. And, in many ways, Petie was the "greatest thing." He made those around him laugh; often spoke in an unintelligible combination of Spanish, English, and, for good measure, the German dialect of Plautdietsch; and was impressive with his consumption of adult beverages when we were out on the town. What's more, he taught me how to not take life too seriously.

Most of the guys around me, I realized, lived with an intensity that I admired—a passion I don't remember from a lot of folks back in high school aside from my closest of friends. Whether it was partying or training, these Ranger wannabes had only one speed: all out.

I will never forget my buddy Felipe on the two-mile and five-mile runs at Airborne School. He was usually slightly faster than me. But on one of the two-milers, I noticed a soldier up ahead limping along with most of his weight on one foot, hobbling like a pirate. The other foot was lifting off of the ground as if it were touching hot coals with each stride. It was Felipe.

"Let's go, Petie," I yelled. "It's only two miles!"

Only later did I learn the crazy dude was running with a severe stress fracture in his foot. Felipe made it through these two graded runs—without complaining once.

As Airborne School came to a close and the next step, Ranger Indoctrination Program (RIP), loomed, I woke up one night with chills. Literal chills. My head ached. In the days to come, I developed a sore throat, loss of appetite, and fever. Desperate, I considered sick call, until I learned that it could threaten to end my dream of becoming an Army Ranger. I had walking pneumonia.

Not, of course, that I was going to tell anybody in a uniform that. Instead, when the weekend arrived, I talked buddies into taking me to an Urgent Care facility about forty-five minutes from Fort Benning.

"Son," a doctor said to me after an exam, "if you were smart, you'd tell your command so that they could either hospitalize you or put you on bed rest."

There is, of course, a difference between "civilian smart" and "soldier smart." To tell anyone back at Benning about my health challenge was to sign a death warrant to my dreams of becoming a Ranger. It's that "weak-deer-in-the-herd" stuff. Green and Fader were like wolves looking to thin the pack; my job was to do everything possible to stay with that pack.

The Rangers had a reputation to uphold. Enemies feared the green-eyed hue of a Ranger platoon moving toward them. And the reason Rangers got to be that formidable was because of how carefully the 75th Ranger Regiment selected their men.

If walking pneumonia was the bad news, the good news was that RIP classes were so full that we were put on a three-week "RIP Hold." While we waited for the "real thing," my walking pneumonia abated and Felipe's foot healed. The delay saved our Ranger lives.

RIP WAS LIKE SUDDENLY HAVING TO PLAY A VIDEO GAME at the "expert" level after only having played it at "beginner." Everything got faster. Tougher. More intense. At a place called Cole Range on Fort Benning's nether regions, I remember picking up a fallen tree and running back and forth across an open field for three hours. Guys were falling down and we'd all but jump over them. Cole Range was a place where Rangers were made—and dreams were killed.

We started with 200 guys. By the time the weeding-out process was over, assuming you survived, the guy to your left and right would not be there; about two out of three wouldn't make it. The physical tests were relentless: Climbing up and down a fifteen-foot barrier. Swimming across a pool—in full gear. Push-ups. Pull-ups. Sit-ups. Runs. Marches. Sometimes in pitch black or after you were pulled from bed. Suddenly, you'd be on your stomach, like an alligator, crawling through a foot of water and mud—in full gear and carrying your rifle.

The pain was so intense that at times you'd find yourself hallucinating amid the Georgia heat. And keep in mind: this was not Army Ranger School. That would come about a year later, if I made it through RIP—and after my first deployment.

Ranger School, which dates back to 1950 at Fort Benning, was attended by anyone in the US military as well as foreign military members. RIP, on the other hand, was only for people seeking to be assigned to the Special Operations force of the 75th Ranger Regiment. Ranger School was tough, no doubt. But it was cake compared to RIP. There were times, over a year later during Mountain Phase of Ranger School where, in the snow, I thought I might fall asleep and be left behind to die.

Fader's counterpart was Staff Sergeant Green, a man with whom I would later serve in Afghanistan. As we waited for the next "event" confined within the walls of the RIP compound, it was decided we'd be given some physical exercise—again. During calisthenics, Green paced between the rows of men doing pushups like the Grim Reaper, looking for someone—anyone—to show even the slightest signs of weakness. He and Fader had one purpose: to take a perfectly capable human and tear him down as if stuffing him through a paper shredder.

"C'mon, Brooks!" he'd yell. "Can't let that little cough of yours be any sort of excuse. Move your ass!"

After hours of destroying us with physical tests and making us question our worth as human beings, Fader, Green, and the rest of the cadre would be charged with determining who was fit for the 75th Ranger Regiment. Who would lead the way in all infantry skills and on a two-pronged battlefield: Iraq and Afghanistan.

It not only takes a special person to become a Ranger, it takes an individual who has the willpower to punish his own body beyond limits he knew existed. Or someone like me, stubborn as a mule. The punishment wasn't something to endure for one day or even one week of misery either. Try six months, minimum, once you made it to your Ranger Battalion. In other words, it wasn't just physical and mental obstacles you had to overcome, you had to do so time and again. It wasn't just strength and smarts, it was endurance. It was like: "Congrats on being assigned to the 75th Ranger Regiment—now meet your executioner. Meet the guy who will make the next six months to a year of your life a test of intestinal fortitude and with some added time in a war zone or two."

My job was not only to survive this course, but to blend in with a group of guys who were some of the toughest humans I would ever meet, guys who were always picked first in the schoolyard football games. Guys who'd been raised in rugged home situations and had gone toe-to-toe with their fathers. Guys who knew becoming a Ranger was the only way they were going to avoid winding up in prison. And a sprinkling of guys like me who were raised by great parents in cozy communities with relatively cushy lives.

What bound us together was our youth. We were young and rambunctious and a bit cocky; to us, the future was the end of whatever day we were trying to get through. Our world was small: Fort Benning and whatever handful of bars we visited nearby. Our pasts were, if not forgotten, put on hold; any political, racial, or ethnic differences didn't apply. Our futures were so foggy that we didn't even stop to think much about what would happen once we actually became Rangers; we were too busy trying just to qualify for that coveted tan beret.

A few months after I'd arrived in Georgia to train, the news came: Pat Tillman, my Ranger hero, had been killed in Afghanistan. It happened on April 22, 2004. I couldn't believe it; to me, it was like Superman dying. *This just couldn't happen.* It shook up a lot of us guys who were going the Option 40 route. *Tillman?*

He was all-everything in football. He was bigger than life. And he had the conscience and heart and integrity to go with it. The absolute Full Meal Deal. *Dead? Impossible.*

We didn't talk much about it, but if the other guys were thinking what I was thinking, then they were trying on a thought more uncomfortable than RIP: *If Tillman could die in war, what did that mean for me—a mere mortal?*

AN OUTSIDER MIGHT THINK STAFF SERGEANT FADER hated life, humans, and even puppies; that he was nothing more than an angry dude. My sense was that he was savvy and smart, and really good at his job of invoking fear into every student. Whenever he was near me during a "smoke session" of physical punishment, I would offer my best chameleon impression. It really was the best survival technique for me to maintain my sanity. *Blend in, Brooks. Don't make a mistake.*

Not that I always did. The late, hot summer in Columbus, Georgia, was like nothing I'd ever experienced. It was in the upper 90s with 100 percent humidity. Awful—and that's coming from a kid who grew up near Sacramento, which is no stranger to heat. But California offers a dry heat, not the Southern heat that leaves you damper than a post-shower towel.

Green walked the rows as if he were the Tasmanian Devil in Army fatigues. Fader was equally wild.

"You!" Fader snapped at me early on. "What's your name? Stand up!"

I froze, hoping he hadn't seen me resting a tad between pushups.

"I said get up!"

I jumped up, snapped my hands behind my back to "parade rest" and yelled, "Brooks, *sergeant!*"

Fader looked me in the eyes.

"Are you quitting?" he rasped in a whisper.

"Negative, sergeant!"

"Private *Brooks*," he said, in a voice for all to hear, "thinks it is okay to put a knee down while the rest of you are doing pushups. I think we should all thank him for the next hour of hell. Can I hear a 'Thank you, Private Brooks, may I have another?'"

"Thank you, Private Brooks," said the entire RIP class, with mock enthusiasm, "may I have another?"

Fader looked at me like I had something growing out of my forehead, and he wanted to kill that thing, whatever it may be. His eyes narrowed, his head tilted ever so slightly.

"Are you going to give them what they want? You can stand here and lead them in pushups until you are rested. Go ahead. *Down!*"

"*Down!*" I said in unison with Fader before dropping flat to the down position and rejoining my classmates.

"Who else wants to take a rest and punish his buddies?" asked Fader. "Anyone? *Up!* All of you are one team. When you have someone weak on your team—people die. This is war, not the fucking Cub Scouts."

He paced, scanned the men, letting it sink in.

"You all will be on a battlefield within months—guaranteed. Some of you will leave this course and be sent directly overseas to join your unit. Someone in this formation may be dead within weeks. We don't have time for you to rest. *Down!* If you are going to wear my tan beret, you will not be weak! *Up!*"

Just for fun, they'd throw in some extra crap because apparently this wasn't tough enough. You'd be on that twelve-mile march in the hottest part of the day and they'd stop you and force you to pushups or sit-ups while cussing you out. You'd be waiting in the meal line, feeling thankful you'd survived another day, and, boom, they'd announce a forced run. *Now.*

"War doesn't happen nine-to-five, men, so get used to having to be 'on' when you least expect it!" Green was famous for, say, punishing the entire group because one guy missed curfew. "*Up!*" he'd yell amid the sleeping throng. "You all get a two-mile run because Snuffy couldn't get home on time!"

If you ran like a two-legged cheetah, boom, you were sent packing. If your idea of strength training was the "downward dog"—bye-bye. If you were an independent worker and refused to be team player—get your passport ready for some godawful assignment like Korea.

In short, if you didn't cut it, you were likely assigned to another airborne-based unit in the United States Army and on your way out of RIP. The instructors would constantly threaten us with "Korea" as our next duty station, which was thought to be the "worst" of infantry duty stations. It wasn't even an airborne unit, which to an airborne-qualified guy, would be shameful. It may have actually been a great assignment, but the fear I felt was real. There was only one greater fear: the fear of failing, period. It was simply not an option.

I hated failing. Whether it was the raging fit that I threw after striking out in little league, or obsessively trying to compete with my younger brother Michael, it was all in the name of winning. Heck—before blowing out my knee, I thought I could make it as a basketball star, despite my lack of height. I was also kind of a wimp. I was the kid with the Pee Wee Herman doll who I'd always bring out to raucous laughter—not realizing until I was a teenager that folks weren't laughing *with* me, but *at* me.

My wimpiness was always driving me to do more. To push harder. Despite my background suggesting that I wouldn't be good at this Ranger stuff, it drove me to push beyond what I perceived to be my physical and mental limits.

When RIP was over, I learned I'd survived, as had my buddies. But the satisfaction of knowing I was going to be a Ranger got lost in the tumult of learning where my buddies and I were headed to begin actual training. There was a no-parents-invited ceremony, just a gathering at which we were allowed to don our glorious tan berets.

The history of the Rangers alone made you feel as if part of something special. Among other places, Rangers scaled the ninety-foot cliffs of Pointe du Hoc on Omaha Beach during the D-day landings in World War II. It was an incident on that day that lead to the Ranger motto: "Rangers Lead the Way." Korea. Vietnam. Grenada. Panama. Afghanistan. Iraq. Rangers have kept leading the way.

Just reading our creed—the first letter of each section spelling out RANGER—gave me goose bumps:

Recognizing that I volunteered as a Ranger, fully knowing the hazards of my chosen profession, I will always endeavor to uphold the prestige, honor, and high esprit de corps of my Ranger Regiment.

Acknowledging the fact that a Ranger is a more elite soldier who arrives at the cutting edge of battle by land, sea, or air, I accept the fact that as a Ranger my country expects me to move further, faster, and fight harder than any other soldier.

Never shall I fail my comrades. I will always keep myself mentally alert, physically strong, and morally straight and I will shoulder more than my share of the task whatever it may be, one-hundred percent and then some.

Gallantly will I show the world that I am a specially selected and well-trained soldier. My courtesy to superior officers, neatness of dress, and care of equipment shall set the example for others to follow.

E-nergetically will I meet the enemies of my country. I shall defeat them on the field of battle for I am better trained and will fight with all my might. Surrender is not a Ranger word. I will never leave a fallen comrade to fall into the hands of the enemy and under no circumstances will I ever embarrass my country.

Readily will I display the intestinal fortitude required to fight onto the Ranger objective and complete the mission, though I be the lone survivor.

RANGERS LEAD THE WAY!

I admit: the idea of wearing the tan beret was cool. I felt a little like an athlete might feel, I supposed, when learning he or she had qualified for the Olympic Trials or was drafted into the NFL. You were among the country's best. And yet I reminded myself: *you haven't proven anything yet, soldier.*

THE LAST STEP WAS TO RECEIVE OUR BATTALION assignments. 1st Battalion was headed for the beach in Savannah, Georgia. 2nd Battalion headed to Fort Lewis, Washington, just south of Seattle. And 3rd Battalion was staying right there at Fort Benning. We had all previously agreed that either 1st or 2nd Battalion were better options, since none of my crew wanted to stay at Benning.

There were rumors that the cadre would tell you to line up into three equal groups and assign you at random, or that they would let you choose a group that you desired, only to switch the entirety of the groups so that no one got their choice of duty station. I gathered with my closest buddies, Felipe, Delong, and Crino, trying to figure out some sort of plan to follow so we might stick together. In the end, Fader gave us instructions on how it would all go down. He pointed to three individual areas of the courtyard.

"1st Battalion go over there, 2nd can go here, and 3rd can go here. Go!"

The scramble of sixty men trying to get into a particular place as fast as possible was hilarious. Like crazed rats, guys smashed into each other as they scurried to their desired spots.

My pals and I all got what we wanted—Fort Lewis. But it didn't take long for the reality to settle in. We had spent six months proving ourselves worthy of being US Army Airborne Rangers. We had learned the skills necessary to be members of the 75th Ranger Regiment.

Now we needed to prove that we were worthy to remain a part of that elite unit.

3

TWO DEATHS
AND A UNICORN

SITREP: 9 months prior to the crash of *Turbine 33*
Seattle, Washington

IT WAS SEPTEMBER 22, 2004, AND WE ARRIVED AT
Seattle-Tacoma International Airport to crisp blue skies and
cotton-ball clouds. Outsiders love to joke about the Pacific
Northwest's weather; "What do they call three days of rain in a
row in Seattle? A weekend." But the fact is the place could be
amazingly beautiful, especially in the summer and early fall,
when we'd arrived.

The landscape was lushly sprinkled with clusters of evergreen
trees. Fingers of Puget Sound waters stretched far and wide
to the west. To the east, 14,410-foot Mount Rainier rose like a
sentry, watching our every move, a beautiful hunk of rock, even
if at this time of year, it needed a fresh coat of paint—the cold,
white, wintry kind. I was in awe of the mountain.

"Hey, Delong, look at this crazy volcano!" I said when we'd first seen it. "Any bets that we will have to climb that baby at some point?"

"No doubt—and that, my friend, is gonna suck."

We were driven through the entrance of the Ranger compound, whose rectangular-shaped layout was surrounded by a ten-foot-high, brown fence that seemed to say to the public: "None of your damn business. Don't even ask." My eyes widened, not that the fort's buildings exuded stunning architecture or that the grounds were better kept than those at Arlington National Cemetery, but just that I was *there*. The feeling was overwhelming. Special. Surreal. For a kid whose athletic career had gone up in flames, it was like some sort of weird rebirth where I'd walked into a hallowed stadium not as a spectator who would be sitting in the stands but as a player who would be on the field.

These were the fields and woods and compounds where people such as Pat Tillman had cut their teeth; it was an honor to be there. At times I would think: *Me? An Army Ranger?*

Once we were familiar with our new work environment, we, of course, had to establish a new play environment: in this case, Cowgirls Inc., a bar with a "Coyote Ugly" theme in the shadow of the Seattle Seahawks' spanking-new CenturyLink Field. It was a forty-five-minute drive up Interstate 5 from Fort Lewis, a hangout that was military-friendly. If Fort Lewis's appearance said, "Don't be poking around here," Cowgirls Inc.'s said pretty much just the opposite: "Gawk at our girls, drink our beer, keep it clean, and spend a helluva lot of money."

We obliged. I mean, hey, if some of the patrons could act a bit stupid, the owners weren't dumb; they knew that girls in cowboy boots dancing atop tables was, next to beer, the best draw. And they were absolutely right.

I hadn't been there long when I started to get to know—well, OK, I learned the name of—one of the bartenders: Heidi. She was a beautiful, spunky, and strong-willed woman. She was just twenty-two, the same age I was. People who say love at first sight is a myth didn't see me fall for her like a blindfolded man stepping into the Grand Canyon. It was one thing to see someone who you think is attractive—another to feel your blood pressure rise and your heart pound in your chest. And still have enough narcissism to think that "there might be a chance." I am a pretty practical guy. But this time, I was completely out of my mind.

For the first time in my life, I felt like I couldn't let a girl get away, which is an interesting notion since I didn't even "have her" in the first place. But I knew I had to get a date with this young woman. She'd grown up in Packwood, a small town in the Big Bottom Valley near White Pass, and moved to Seattle soon after she'd graduated from high school. She was gorgeous, inside and out.

"Brooksie, aren't you playing up a couple of divisions with this gal?" said Peters. "Like maybe three?"

I looked at him very seriously. Then replied with my typical smart-ass response, "Send me in, coach."

I proceeded to "bravely" order a few drinks and politely pester her for a date. I couldn't deny that she was beyond me. But, you see, that's exactly why she intrigued me; just like Forrest was naïve enough to think he could wind up with Jenny, I was "Gump enough" to believe I could win over Heidi. When I'd enlisted, I wasn't going to settle for being regular army. And there was nothing regular about her. She was elite. She was my "Option 40"; one look at her and I was looking beyond everyday infantry and shooting for the Rangers.

Peters started to call her The Unicorn, based not on appearance but on the more mysterious meaning of the word: "something unusual, rare, unique." I was absolutely enamored by this amazing human being and, me being me, I made fun of myself with future dreams, one of which depicted me marrying her.

I turned to one of my Ranger buddies, Justin Hatfield.

"Hatty, will you be my best man when I marry 'The Unicorn?'" He rolled his eyes.

While I was plummeting off the Grand Canyon's South Rim, I'm not sure Heidi had even fallen off a curb in love with me. In fact, I'm quite sure she'd forgotten my name, if she'd even remembered it for a nanosecond. One night at the bar, I, as always, continued my offensive maneuvers.

"Heidi, maybe we should chat sometime when you aren't working," I said. "Where's the best place to call you?"

She smiled—*oh, those beautiful dimples!*—and put her hands on her hips. "Sorry," she said, "I have a boyfriend."

I wasn't deterred in the least. The following weekend, I was back.

"Maybe we could grab dinner sometime."

She batted her almond-shaped eyes. My knees went weak.

"I have a boyfriend. *Still.*"

"That's nice," I said. "What phone number might *he* use to reach you?"

"Sorry."

The next weekend I was back again. Again, she nixed my dinner suggestion.

"You know," I said, "it doesn't have to be dinner. Lunch works."

She nodded her head—*beautiful brownish-blonde hair*—as if to applaud the effort, but the only numbers she was giving me were the ones on my bar tab.

Remember, though, I was analytical. A letter-of-the-law guy. What I hadn't heard, in response to my questions, was "no." Weekend after weekend, I kept sending word patrols across her front lines, hoping for a soft spot that I might exploit. The absence of "no" energized my quest for "yes." In another nod to *Dumb and Dumber,* she was clearly "telling me there's a chance."

LIFE BACK AT FORT LEWIS ITSELF HAD BEGUN WITH A more sobering start. (There was nothing "sober" about Cowgirls Inc.) We had unloaded our gear. Without a care in the world, Delong, Crino, and I instinctively started joking about war. Peters was usually the funniest one of the bunch; he routinely ripped off one-liners that would make a constipated DMV clerk laugh. But I noticed he just kept stacking bags, with no emotion, no response, no words. He was in "the zone." In his own world. Or perhaps feeling the compound's energy. I couldn't be certain why the usually off-the-wall kid suddenly went quiet, but it gave me the heebie-jeebies. Like deep down, he knew something we didn't. Or didn't know it but *felt* it.

As we gathered our gear in the grass-covered quad of 2nd Ranger Battalion, the Non-Commissioned Officer in Charge (NCOIC) welcomed us—well, not the flowers-and-hugs sort of welcome, but you get the idea. The uneasy feeling I'd gotten after watching Peters go stone-cold quiet lurked over my shoulder like a sky-high vulture, its eyes riveted to my back. Something just wasn't right. And then I understood why. Peters, it turned out, had overheard that there had been a soldier casualty, but did the correct thing and kept it to himself.

"We are on lockdown," the NCO told us soon after we'd unpacked our bags. "We had a casualty last night in Iraq—and we are still in the process of notifying the family. That means no cell phones, no leaving, no talking. *Nothing!* You will stay in your company area until we give you word that the family is notified. His name is Ranger Stahl. He was killed by an IED [Improvised Explosive Device]."

Shit. That wasn't how our introduction to Ranger life was supposed to have gone. My giddy anticipation dropped like a bird shot from the sky. Then I remembered: *It's not about you, soldier. In this case, it's about Private 1st Class Nathan Stahl of Charlie Company.*

Whatever invincibility I felt walking into Fort Lewis had disappeared, whatever wind filled my sails suddenly stopped. Once the lockdown was over, and we were cleared to use electronics again, I did what I always do. I called my dad, my go-to guy, a huge part of my life. He was always there to listen, offer good advice, and occasionally put me in my place when I needed it.

When I was a kid, we'd shared a love for golf; he put a set of clubs in my hands when I was nine or ten and invited his game to be my game. I accepted. Many a weekend, we'd wake early and head to the golf course for a round. He taught me the basics of the golf swing and I picked it up pretty fast. By the time I was ten, I was taking lessons, by the time I was a teenager I was pretty damn good. Still, Dad would kick my butt most of the time. I did beat him on occasion, but it wasn't until my teen years—and even then he joked that he'd "let me win." I cherished those weekends on the golf course. Not only was I fiercely competitive, but I enjoyed the time with my dad.

But now I wasn't calling him from the golf course to ask for a ride home, I was calling him to tell him that on my first day at Fort Lewis, we'd already had a death-triggered lockdown.

"Dad, a Ranger was killed last night," I said into my Razr flip phone. "And he was in my new company."

Silence. He was clearly at a loss for words. "That, uh, that's not good. I hate to hear that . . ." he paused for seconds that seemed like minutes. "I hope they got the guy responsible." I didn't know the answer but felt the need to leave the conversation on a lighter note.

"Dad, you *know* they did. Rangers don't take that shit from anyone." This was enough to move the conversation on. We had some closure—for now.

SO, THE INTRODUCTION AT FORT LEWIS HAD A MORE sinister feel to it than at Cowgirls Inc.: fear. Fear of what awaited us. Fear of the unknown. And fear of the old standard, failure.

A bit more about that failure. There were no guarantees here. At any point, any one of us could be "released for standards." We called it "RFS'd." And it was my worst fear. Even thinking about being sent to a regular army unit because I couldn't cut it felt like death.

All this created strange relationships. Deep down, we needed each other's support; we were like helpless orphans, thrown into a live-or-die environment. We would stomp our buddy's face in the mud if it meant helping us get over an obstacle-course barrier. All in the name of competition.

"It was a complete Alpha environment," my buddy Hatfield later told an interviewer. "You were constantly cutting your fellow brother down. Any sign of weakness and you're out. So, it had to be this way." And he was absolutely correct. We would smash each other in the face in competition, then buy each other a drink later that same night and act like "friends for life." It was a brotherhood that was no different from the relationship I had with my own brother. We could be in fisticuffs one moment, then plotting the destruction of our enemies the next.

In the early-goings at Ft. Lewis, at headquarters company, I looked toward my three closest friends—Delong, Peters, and Crino—my face creased with smugness and my head nodding slightly.

"So," I said, "this is where we learn to slay terrorists, huh?"

"No," said Delong, the wisest and most mature of the bunch. "This is where we learn to treat them with respect and teach them the errors of their ways—*then* kill them."

The NCO interrupted our wayward thoughts.

"OK, privates, you're about to meet your new company, or at least the guys who are not currently deployed who are in your company." Currently, 2nd Ranger Battalion was split into company-sized elements and spread between Afghanistan and Iraq. With two wars raging simultaneously, it was common to have a single Ranger Battalion split amongst the two theaters. All we knew was that the majority of our battalion was due home within weeks; they would go on leave to recover from their most recent war-zone deployment. We would not go on leave since we had just arrived.

"I will read off your names by company," he said—and started to do just that. I heard none of the names until it was one I recognized, a guy I knew. "Delong—Bravo Company." *OK, so we knew where one of our small close-knit group members was headed.* Bravo Company was located on the northeast area of the compound. "Crino—Charlie Company." At eighteen, Crino was the youngest of our crew and the most energetic. He was tall and lanky, like a baby giraffe only with puppy-dog eyes. We would always tease him about his eyes, because he had the eyelashes that girls would kill for. "Crino, just bat your eyes at the ladies and you are golden," we would always remind him. He never seemed to mind.

"Brooks—Charlie Company." I looked at Crino and whipped him a quick fingerpoint to acknowledge our same-company assignment. He nodded and returned a small fist pump. We had become accustomed to not standing out from the crowd. We had learned that if you brought attention to yourself, you would have to deal with whatever came from it. The good. The bad. The endless pushups.

"Peters—Charlie Company."

Yes! The Three Amigos destined for Charlie Company locked eyes and nodded in unison. *Let's do this.* I was relieved to know that I would have familiar faces in Charlie Company. Even Charlie Company guys who'd already arrived before us quickly became friends, chief among them a kid named Devin Peguero-Cardenas, twenty, from LA, specifically Chino Hills. He'd enlisted a few months before I had. I got to know him a bit when we took in a Seattle Mariners baseball game in September, the kind of thing we almost never got to do.

Because of a room shortage, a bunch of us slept in a common area. That meant putting up cots each night—and nobody was more committed to that task than Peguero. He was a total team guy. Hundred percent extrovert. Always a smile on his face. Natural leader. From a huge Hispanic family, much like my mother's side of the family back home. And he absolutely welcomed me into the Charlie Company family.

There was nothing selfish or standoffish about him. Instantly it was: "You're in Charlie Company, you're my brother. You're family." He was a close friend of Hatfield, who would also become a close friend of mine. Peguero was one of those "old soul" folks, wise beyond his years. I liked him from the get-go— and I think I had pretty good intuition about people.

Rangers, I'd learned, seemed to come in three varieties:

A. "Strong Rangers." Mainly former athletes. Guys who were stud athletes in high school, maybe even college, and wanted to make sure everyone knew it. They arrived with loads of confidence, were used to winning, and tended to have plenty of "followers."

B. "Smart Rangers." Guys who were never going to get by simply on their strength, so relied on their brains. Tended to not ruffle feathers. Did as they were told. And found ways to help the team. I suppose I'd have been classified as a Smart Ranger. I'd always prided myself in being able to pick things up quickly and the military had zillions of things you needed to "pick up." To be sure, though I'd "beefed up" twenty pounds to 185, nobody mistook me for a Strong Ranger.

C. "Lone Rangers." These were the "tweeners" who almost defied labeling. They might have been boneheads who simply didn't listen and obey. They might have been lone wolves who talked the team game but didn't walk it. They got through on their smarts—some had been engineers and lawyers in earlier lives—but sometimes could be dumb as fence posts. When they tried to lead, they'd often look back and find nobody following them—except for a few guys who wanted to thwart them for being screw-ups and putting the unit in danger.

I suppose I had a touch of "lone ranger," not because I didn't row the same direction—or as hard—as the others, but because I was a fiercely independent thinker. Ask some of my buddies which historical figures they'd want to share a meal with, and most would include at least one *Playboy* Playmate of the Month.

Me? I'd choose Albert Einstein (one of the most brilliant minds of all time); Thomas Jefferson (I'd love to pick his brain about the founding of the United States); and Elon Musk (I love how big he thinks; I think I have at least a little of that in me, minus the billions of dollars, of course).

One more thing about Rangers: All are airborne-qualified. But contrary to popular belief, attendance and passing Army Ranger school does *not* make you an Airborne Ranger. To call yourself an Airborne Ranger, you must serve in the 75th Ranger Regiment. A Ranger School graduate is considered "Ranger qualified," but to call themselves a Ranger is like calling someone with an accounting degree an accountant.

AT LEWIS, WE TRAINED TWELVE TO FOURTEEN HOURS A day, almost every day. Because you have to get things right. Captain Work, a mountain of a man, demanded it of us. He was a former Army football captain and middle linebacker who weighed probably sixty pounds more than I did. He demanded we get things right, critiquing us endlessly.

"Men, your breach is too damn slow!" he'd yell. Or: "Your rifles aren't engaged!" Or: "Hug the wall some more! Start the barrel of our gun at this point, not that one!" He wanted it perfect. Otherwise, someone dies.

The autumn of 2004 gave way to winter; the Pacific Northwest's infamous rains began turning Fort Lewis cold and wet and gray. Meanwhile, the training cycle for our next deployment was in full swing. Each Ranger platoon was at one of the numerous training exercises. One platoon would be at the close-quarter combat range in which we practiced room clearing and marksmanship. Another platoon would be working on battle drill scenarios. Another would be practicing what to do if we were attacked while in vehicles. Another would be doing a combination of close-quarters combat room clearing and clearing a city street.

On December 16, we were winding up for the day—we'd been working on vehicle movements—when a squad leader asked us to listen up.

"Before you knuckleheads head over to your respective company area, we have some business." He scanned all of our eyes, more than happy to let the silence stir our souls and leave us just a tad befuddled. When he looked my way, it seemed as if he were staring right through my eyes and into the back of my skull. I felt chills—why, I had no idea. Almost all Ranger NCOs, I would come to find, learn to deliver this glare as part of their repertoire. For now it was relatively new—and unsettling.

"We had a casualty," he said. "Three Charlie has a guy en route to Madigan Army Medical Hospital."

"What happened?" someone asked.

"Live-fire accident. Sounds bad. I will let you know when we hear more."

Shit! Only three months into my Ranger career and we had another guy down. This time, right here in training. I was not only disappointed and upset, I was livid. I threw my tactical shooting gloves into my open bag in front of me out of frustration. We had been on ranges up to sixteen hours a day for the past week and I was at my wits' end. I was physically exhausted from the grueling training and emotionally drained from knowing that one of our own was on his way to the ER with a probable gunshot wound.

"Heard it's a new guy," a fellow Ranger said.

Great, I'm a "new guy." Peters was a new guy. Hatfield—my best friend, squad mate, and roommate—was a new guy. Would we, too, soon be headed for the ER—or worse?

That's what makes being a soldier different from being a civilian. With exceptions, of course—cops, surgeons, and guys welding joints on the fifty-ninth floor of a new skyscraper—people screw up in their job and the consequences are small. A customer at the big-box hardware store gets sold one-inch PVC when he needed two-inch. Or the couple at a restaurant gets served a sweet Riesling instead of a dry Riesling. In the military, on the other hand, someone screws up and they either wind up in the ER or in a flag-draped casket being flown back home in the belly of a C-17.

To take my mind off the latest casualty, I thought about the wiry and quick-witted Hatfield, a fellow Northern Californian from San Jose. We shared a third-story corner room, 336, in 1st Platoon's area of operation. We would often greet each other with a fist bump and a chant of "THREE-THREE-SIX" in our deepest voices as we attempted to imitate Ice Cube's famous, "Yea! Yea!" Our room was a ten-foot-by-ten-foot box. It was artificially separated in the middle by a large wardrobe cabinet: Justin and his bed on one side of the wardrobe, mine on the other. In other words, nothing that was going to show up on Joanna Gaines's *Magnolia* magazine cover.

Justin wasn't just my roommate or even a friend; he was more like a brother. When I needed him, he would be *there*. When he needed me, I would be *there*. We teased each other constantly.

"Hey, Hatty," I'd say. "Get over here and make me a sammich." He would pucker his lips and quickly respond with, "Only if you give me a kiss first."

We could be doing some serious training in a shoot house, yet never stop antagonizing each other—one of us giving the other a hard time for no reason whatsoever. Followed by a snarky response, with both of us being oddly happy about the outcome.

We both enjoyed some good rap music, and he loved pop singer Kelly Clarkson. Me? I was saving my heart for The Unicorn.

Now, a serious mood settled over Charlie Company like winter fog. Shortly after word came down of the accident, I found Hatfield sitting in a Humvee.

"Ya hear?" he said. "Heard he was pronounced dead."

It was mid-December, getting dark, and cold. I could see his breath. He leaned over and just said it like that. The kid who'd been injured in the live-fire incident. Dead.

"Can't believe it," he said.

He had his elbows on his knees and hands on his forehead—almost as if he knew something I didn't. Like there was more to this story.

"What's going on, Hatty?"

He slowly turned and looked me in the eyes. He took a deep breath, blew out, then pursed his lips. My stomach was knotting like a tightly twisted towel.

"It was Peguero," he said softly.

My hands fell to my knees, then I instinctively folded over. Head down, both hands over my face. *This couldn't have happened.*

"Seriously? Devin?"

"Overheard it from HQ."

Peguero, the guy who'd welcomed me into Charlie Company like I'd belonged all the time. Hatfield was great friends with Devin. They had both arrived at 2nd Ranger Battalion a month before I did. Peguero also had a close connection to Peters. They were roommates.

"Son of a bitch," I said. "What the hell happened?"

A simple error had led to his death. A target had been misplaced on a range simulating a city street—a target that was misplaced on a shared wall. When both rooms were being occupied and Ranger fire teams engaged the simulated enemy, a 5.56mm round pierced the shared wall and hit Peguero on the other side. Tragic as it was, and it was tragic, Peguero's death resulted in all of us hunkering down and making sure that we were training hard, but safe. We'll never know, but I firmly believed Peguero's sacrifice protected the rest of us in significant ways. We'd learned from his death. His legacy continued on to keep us all safe for many deployments to come.

Naturally, Hatfield and Peters were taking the death hard. So was I.

The *Seattle Times* ran a story about it—ACCIDENTAL SHOOTING CLAIMS LIFE OF SOLDIER—that told us some things we had and hadn't known. We knew he had been awarded the National Defense Service Medal, the Global War on Terrorism Service Medal, the Army Service Ribbon, and the Parachutist Badge. We didn't know that he'd been pronounced dead shortly after arrival at Madigan Army Medical Center. Or that according to military statistics, approximately 250 soldiers, sailors, and airmen are killed accidentally each year in noncombat duty. When you're training for war, you train exactly as you fight. Naturally, that's going to lead to some deaths.

"Hatty" and a few others later flew to Los Angeles to do the flag presentation for the family at the memorial service. What he experienced blew him away: "unconditional love for us all, despite what happened," he told me. The family embraced him without reservation.

"You could argue we killed their son in training," he said. "But they still loved us. They could have blamed us. But there we are in his backyard, at a barbecue, and they are welcoming us with open arms." I think it was because they knew we loved their son. Their connection to us gave them a connection to him.

He'd, in essence, given his life for us; they knew we would have done the same for him. And that was the brotherhood. We would all risk it all to help one another. It was what made us different.

I can't say how Peguero's death affected the others. But I know it crushed Hatty, Peters, and me.

"I thought we were invincible," Hatty later told me. "Nothing could touch us."

And I'd thought the same thing.

Part of it was how it had happened. Not in a war zone at the hands of the enemy, but right here on our training grounds—at the hands of our own guys. This was frickin' *training*. If this kind of thing happened right here at home, what might happen when we headed for our first deployment, to Afghanistan?

4

TO AFGHANISTAN

SITREP: 3 months prior to the crash of *Turbine 33*
Somewhere over the Atlantic Ocean

November 2004: Training with my squad on Fort Lewis, WA. We had many long nights getting ready for Afghanistan.

THE C-17 THRUMMED LIKE A BELT SANDER. IT WAS April 4, 2005, seven months after I'd first arrived at Fort Lewis. The 2nd Ranger Battalion's Charlie Company was headed for Afghanistan. It was, we'd been told, a four-month deployment.

Basically, any Ranger unit is expected to be ready to be sent to any square inch on the Earth—and be there within twenty-four hours. I loved that "firefighter" feeling, that sense that if there was trouble, we got to help quell that trouble. Whatever it was. Wherever it was. Whenever it came down.

As I lay face up on the floor of the giant plane, I couldn't help but think about my family back home. *What are my parents thinking right now? They have no idea that I am on a plane, let alone one headed for Afghanistan.* We were not allowed to give out exact deployment dates to family. It was for everyone's protection, but mostly to keep the enemy on their toes. You grow up and it's instinctive to let your parents know where you're going; now I was headed to war nearly 7,000 miles away and I couldn't say a word.

I knew that my mother wouldn't be sleeping much when she realized that I was off fighting a war. When I was a kid she'd worry if I was an hour late home from a dance or a game; now there was a chance I wouldn't be coming home for up to six months. I had the best mom in the world—still do—and when I was eight, I played a little game of hide and seek with her that she would never forget. In a large department store, I talked my brother into hiding with me in a clothes rack while Mom picked school clothes for us. We hid so well that she had to alert the manager, who shut down the store, got on the loudspeaker and said, "We have two lost children, young boys about eight and six with brown hair."

That was short-term panic on Mom's part. Having a son at war, I feared, would be far worse. I also had to face the reality that I might not be coming home, period. The deaths of Stahl and Peguero were stark reminders that, whether in war or training for war, the ammo was real, the enemy real, the stakes high.

Once we were on board the plane, our company commander briefed us, his voice loud to overcome the sound of the engines.

"OK, men, we are off to bring the fight to the enemy," he said. "Relax—and get some rest. We will be operational shortly after landing. Meanwhile, Doc will issue you something to help you get some rest if you need it. See you in twenty-four hours."

It was among my life's murkier days, like opening your eyes underwater while swimming in Puget Sound. Cold. Uncertain. Clouded by all sorts of emotional sediment. The future, my future, was as undefined as it had ever been. I knew little about where we were going and what, specifically, I would be doing. I only knew we were going to war. And, so, between an hour of sleep here and there, my mind found its way to the past.

I don't think any of us had forgotten about Peguero. Death, you realized, was non-discriminatory. It came for the good guys, too, Peguero clearly among them. And it came when you least expected it: not in some high-pitched battle but in an ordinary day of training, a Thursday afternoon in mid-December. Was it coming for the rest of us? For me? What the hell had I gotten myself into?

I knew little of death. The one loss that had stuck with me had been a grandfather who I had admired greatly. I was thirteen. Bruce Brooks died of prostate cancer at the age of sixty-nine. On September 28, 1996, I lost a role model. A family member. A man who inspired me to succeed in life. His passing hit me hard. A sucker punch to my soul.

Nobody could do a Donald Duck impression like my grandfather, but even though he could make his grandchildren laugh, he was intense—a hard-charging executive with a penthouse office suite near downtown Sacramento. And he was successful. He took a huge risk in starting an oil company in 1964. He didn't have an inheritance. He didn't win the lottery. Instead, he busted his ass, building it from the ground up. I admired that. I hoped to do the same someday—build a business of my own.

My grandfather knew the value of hard work and of building a team, surrounding himself with people as passionate and purposeful as he was. Among them was a young-buck attorney by the name of Anthony M. Kennedy, a Stanford and Harvard Law School grad who, like my grandfather, had great drive and great vision. And he followed that vision. Kennedy would ultimately serve thirty years as a US Supreme Court justice.

In 1987, when Kennedy was nominated to the court by President Ronald Reagan, he was subjected to an unprecedentedly thorough investigation of his background but passed without major difficulty. That was a testament to his character and the way he lived his life. In our family, Kennedy had always been this larger than life guy. In fact, my father so admired Kennedy that he named his first-born son—*me*—for the man. He could rankle both conservatives and liberals by seeking the one thing that can cross any party line—the truth. I loved that he pleased and pissed off both sides of the political spectrum equally. That, I believe, is a strength, not a weakness.

Not that I knew any of this back when my grandfather died when I was just thirteen years old. All I knew is that Kennedy was a great friend of my now-gone grandfather, at whose funeral, in 1996, I cried hard and often. Afterward, my grandfather's remains were placed in a cemetery's "Court of Honor" that was reserved for military veterans; he had been a boatswain in the navy.

It was at the burial that Kennedy, having been on the Supreme Court for eight years by this time, pulled my younger brother, Michael, and me aside. He shook our hands and shared his condolences for our loss. He squatted down to our level and looked the two of us straight in the eyes.

"Your grandfather," he said, "was a great man and will be greatly missed. All of us lost someone special." Kennedy then proceeded to distract us from our grief by walking us over to the vehicle that he'd arrived in. It was none other than a Humvee. He and the Secret Service guys in suits let us explore the up armored military vehicle inside and out. It was cool beyond belief. My brother Michael and I kept admiring it while glancing back and forth with giant smiles on our faces. Both of us thinking about how cool it would be to drive one as a soldier. I will never forget how Justice Kennedy took the time to comfort us in our time of grief. His integrity and compassion in that moment really stuck with me decades later.

After my grandfather's burial, I came home and lay face down on my bed on what I would remember as the saddest day of my life. It's hard to explain how difficult it was for me to overcome this death. I would sit and cry in the laundry room, using the sound of the washer or dryer to hide my meltdown from my family. It was a defining moment in my life. A moment that I realized that death was real and painful.

DAY BECAME NIGHT, NIGHT BECAME DAY, NOT THAT ANY of us noticed; the plane had no windows. This was no sightseeing trip. This was war—and had been for nearly four years. The ashes of the Twin Towers had hardly cooled when President George W. Bush, on October 7, 2001, launched, along with the United Kingdom, Operation Enduring Freedom. It was a euphemistic name for what really amounted to a desire to find, and kill, Osama Bin Laden, the founder of the militant organization, al-Qaeda, and his minions, the Taliban. Bin Laden, it was believed, had masterminded the 9/11 attacks. He was a ruthless underworld leader who'd been banished from the country where he was born, Saudi Arabia, and had found a foothold—and a following—among a segment of Afghanistan's equally corrupt young men itching to fight.

By 2005, he was still on the loose. What had once been a NATO coalition of more than forty countries that initially came together to stamp out such evil was basically now US and allied Afghan government troops battling al-Qaeda insurgents, and those of another such coalition, the Taliban. Yes, other nations were still involved and present, but the US was doing most of the heavy lifting with our British counterparts doing their work in the south end of the country.

Unlike past wars, the US's involvement in Afghanistan hadn't been a surge of large Army or Marine forces. Instead, it had been prosecuted by Special Operations forces from all the services, along with Navy and Air Force tactical power, Afghan Northern Alliance soldiers, and the CIA. Among those Special Operations forces was the 2nd Ranger Battalion's Charlie Company, of which I was part.

BY NOW, HATFIELD, CRINO, AND PETERS WERE THE closest friends of mine headed to Afghanistan with the same 1st Platoon of Charlie Company. As if we'd been a handful of corks dropped in a stream, the rest of my buddies had been funneled down different channels, gone different directions or, as in the case of Peguero, been permanently held up.

I was a tangle of confidence and fear. And, like my buddies, anxious to fight. Wait, that's putting it too mildly. I was young and cocky and absolutely convinced I was going overseas to kill a bunch of terrorists, come home, and party.

But it didn't turn out that way. Not at all.

5

WELCOME TO WAR

SITREP: 3 months before the crash of *Turbine 33*
Bagram Airfield, Afghanistan

WHEN OUR WHEELS TOUCHED DOWN MY ADRENALINE
spiked up. This was what I'd been waiting for: a chance to put
into play everything I'd learned since joining the 75th Ranger
Regiment. A chance to test myself. A chance to bring some good
to the world, by rooting out some of the bad. And that meant
killing the enemy.

Does that sound crass? Maybe. But the attack on America on
9/11 was a vicious line in the sand. You could either pretend the
bad guys didn't exist and risk having them do something like
that again. Or, as if they were rats in the basement, you could get
rid of them. Let me be clear: the goal wasn't to kill. The goal was
to protect our own—our country, our way of life, and our people

in combat. But killing was usually necessary to do that—a means to an end, a just end.

The plane teemed with testosterone—and more than a fair amount of bravado. Like every unit, we thought we were the best group of warriors ever assembled. (Never mind that half of us had never fought.) You just had to be that way, that confident. And every guy within that unit had to thirst for that moment where, under fire, he could prove himself and save all our asses. (Until, I supposed, that moment came and he wanted to be anyone *but* that guy!) Generally speaking, though, we weren't looking the other way.

When the door was popped open to debark the plane at Bagram Airfield on this early-April day, the Afghan heat blasted us like dragon's breath.

"Holy shit," I heard someone lament. "Where's the A/C when you need it?"

This was heat that you not only felt, but *saw,* on the horizon, it hovered over the brown earth like a literal heat wave, a hue of draconian haze that seemed to dare us to survive in its midst.

As we made our way down the steps, Sergeant Jones slapped me on the back with his usual over-the-top force.

"Welcome, Brooks, to Earth's butthole," he said. "Everything that sucks about life is here. Now let's go get it on with some bad dudes."

Jones was never one to hide his feelings. I *was* fully capable, a character trait I suppose I inherited from a father who rarely showed his emotional cards. But I also knew the difference between a private and sergeant, and happily played the game.

"Roger that, sergeant. Let's go kick some bad-guy ass."

We were all like that, a bunch of young men full of piss and vinegar, tired of training and anxious to be tested, bored with video games and ready for real-life warfare. Alas, the first few weeks were hardly the stuff we were all set to embrace. It was slow. *Really* slow. Occasionally, we'd gather for what was known as a "poop" meeting—like much in the army, the name made no sense—in which a leader disseminated information from a higher command about the task at hand. Seldom was that info anything even the least bit intriguing.

In fact, about the most exciting thing we did early on in Afghanistan involved a photo shoot, after some joint training on the tarmac of Bagram Airfield, with the guys from 160th Special Operations Aviation Regiment and their MH-47 helicopter. Only later would we glance at those photos with a pain and regret that we could have never imagined.

Otherwise, little was going on. I had plenty of time on my hands, so occasionally threw a football around, spent an inordinate amount of time at the gym, and shot an occasional email to The Unicorn in Seattle—yes, she had given me her email address. Her casual replies were usually "how's-the-weather?" stuff that didn't inspire me with confidence and that I wasn't allowed to answer—to protect us from possible information leaks to the bad dudes. A cynic would have given up. Not me. *Are you kidding me? She is e-mailing me back. Deep down, she knows I'm The One!*

We trained regularly at the range outside of the base in Bagram. Our marksmanship became incredible. On a shooting course we built ourselves in the desert, our guys could pick off the equivalent of a coin while moving and shooting across a room. Sergeant First Class Congdon would awe us as the senior man in our platoon. We ran. We shot. We ran and shot at the same time. We walked through a helicopter crash recovery with PJs, what we would do if one of our birds went down—even though such scenarios hardly ever happened. We learned how to handle dead bodies. How to recover certain equipment that would need recovering. How to dismantle and destroy the remaining parts of the bird. Even how to use tools such as the "jaws of life." And we had honed our combat craft.

If we got into a firefight before going home, we would win. I think we all believed that. Our platoon had an abundance of additional training on this deployment that made us one of the most lethal platoons in all of the 75th Ranger Regiment.

THE WAR IN AFGHANISTAN WAS CHANGING FOR US troops. Direct counter terrorism warfighting was down, counterinsurgency—"hearts and minds" war—was up. Our fellow American forces in the region were to interact often with the local population as allies rather than forcefully fight our way to victory. Operation Enduring Freedom was in full swing, and action for units such as mine, Charlie Company of 2nd Ranger Battalion, had slowed to a virtual standstill. Nobody liked it. But for now, it was what it was. The counter terror operations were still occurring, but in far fewer operations and not only by Special Operations forces as they were in the recent past.

There are, you quickly learn, two dimensions to fighting a war: one is geography, the other is political. How do you even begin to explain the geography of this northeast region of Afghanistan, in the eastern Kunar Province? Perhaps by saying anyone who pictures only desert and heat are way off. It's mountainous. It's rugged. It's blazing hot in the summer and teeth-chattering cold in the winter. It's mysterious. It's totally foreign—at times, it looks like you're on the friggin' moon—and at times, it's beautiful.

Depending on what geographer you trust, Afghanistan is in either central or south Asia, a landlocked country bordered by Pakistan (southern and eastern borders), Iran (western border), and Turkmenistan, Uzbekistan, Tajikistan, and even a sliver of China (northern border).

The political side of this war involved winning civilians to our side instead of the enemy's side. We needed them; they needed us. We needed their help—largely to root out Taliban fighters and to protect our own guys. They needed us—to give them the security from the likely Taliban backlash. But theory and practice are two different things. It didn't matter how much we told them that we were in their country not only to protect our country's freedom but to protect their own, we could lose their trust in the snap of two fingers. This wasn't a war against the people, it was a war for the people.

Say we accidentally killed a family of civilians in a firefight with the Taliban. Or disrespected the local people's customs. Or bullied our way through a town with no regard for whose town it was. That wouldn't just represent bad public relations, but it would make it all the more difficult for us to get our jobs done. We needed the civilians' understanding of what anyone with half a brain could see was true: we were the good guys and the Taliban were the bad guys. We had come to put down terrorists who cared nothing for the lives of others, be they Afghans or Americans. Nothing else. We hadn't come to blow up mosques or convert anyone from their Muslim ways. We had come only to protect the freedom we Americans valued so highly and free an oppressed population.

But if I understood the importance of the bridge-building here, I had a hard time reconciling that this was the best use of our Ranger unit. I mean, come on, I hadn't spent the last fourteen months of my life training to be a Peace Corps Volunteer. (Which, by the way, I support 100 percent.) That's not who we were as soldiers. We were here to fight.

Sending out Special Operations soldiers to try to win the hearts and minds of another country's civilians seemed to me like sending professional kickboxers door-to-door to sell Girl Scout cookies. The effort was noble but was that group the best fit for the job? "Nation building" is important, necessary, and difficult. It just wasn't the best fit for who we were as Rangers—that's all I'm saying. That's probably why we were mostly non-operational.

We knew our Islamic enemy—political extremists—was ruthless, determined, and cagy. We might have believed that they were nuts for ignoring the virtues of freedom and crazy for how brutally they treated even their fellow Afghans; they favored public executions, cut off the hands of thieves, and treated women with scorn, not allowing them to go to school beyond the age of ten and requiring that they wear burkas to hide their faces. But we also were aware that they knew the land far better than we did. We knew that when we were ten-year-old kids, fawning over Michael Jordan and listening to hip-hop, our opponents were learning to fire machine guns and lay down ambushes. And we knew every interaction would likely come down to one thing: resolve.

Week after week, we trained like crazy and, when passing through villages to get to our ranges, offered our tough-guy look, without being overly aggressive. War had been fought in and around here for years, but we never saw a body; Muslims believed that if you weren't buried within twenty-four hours, you lost your chance to enter Paradise. Amid such different customs, we did our best to be goodwill ambassadors as we drove through Bagram, even if it did not seem to fit our job descriptions.

The heat threatened to fry us. The eagerness to fight morphed to anxiety. Days grew longer, tempers shorter. Pretty soon, some of us started accepting the fact that our deployment might be a complete shut out, that we might be sent home with only barely getting off the base. This is unheard of for a Special Operations deployment.

Most of us liked each other. Most. Remember how I said there were Strong Rangers, Smart Rangers, and Lone Rangers? A couple months into our unpleasant stay in Afghanistan, I'd had enough of one guy who belonged in the latter category. He was just a screw-up, a guy who didn't uphold the spirit of the Rangers to bust our asses in order to make the unit strong. As time went on, it was clear he didn't care about anyone beyond himself, or he was just bad at his job. Either way—I tried to ignore it, but he kept giving half-ass efforts that wound up meaning the rest of us had to compensate for him.

One day he had repeatedly failed to clear a building correctly. He was jumping in front of people, stopping in doorways, and making himself a liability in every way possible. I'd wasted enough words of warning on the dude over the last few months. And now my leaders were telling us that we would all be punished for his screw ups. My pot boiled over. Only one thing was going to get through to this guy—and I delivered the message in the form of a right hook to his eye. Where that came from, I had no idea. Still don't. I was the kid who got picked on while growing up, not the kid picking on others. But I rationalized that I was doing it for the good of the team. And, really, I *was*.

My Platoon Sergeant, SFC Congdon might have agreed. He looked at me with a stern face, cracked a smirk, and boomed his message.

"Brooks," he said. "Never again. You can't be fighting with your own guys. Now get back to work."

He did everything but wink at me to let me know he approved.

"Roger that, sergeant!"

LEAVE NO MAN BEHIND

Deep down, I'm sure he was celebrating 100%, as if I'd done what he'd wished he could have done. And I never spent a nano-second thinking I'd overstepped my bounds. It had to be done. The guy was on his way out of the unit the very next day. Not sure if he quit or was fired. But justice was served. He didn't belong.

SITREP: June 28th, 2005
Special Forces Compound, Bagram Airfield, Afghanistan

WAR FIGHTING IS LIKE BEING AN ANESTHESIOLOGIST: ninety percent boredom and ten percent meaningful work. I am not trying to minimize the great work of anesthesiologists, but after eleven weeks, guys were getting crazy with boredom. Guys would pull out their cots and literally sunbathe in preparation for impressing the ladies back home. Others would be playing Tiger Woods golf on their PlayStation or Xbox. And everyone was working out in the gym on multiple occasions each day.

Then, one day in late June—a day that, of course, looked a helluva lot like all the others—Sergeant Jones came running past us with what looked to be a sense of urgency. I knew something was up.

"Get to the hooch!" he yelled. "A bird went down!"

My feelings instantaneously worked their way into a knotted mess. This meant action, an end to the boredom. But it also meant heavy casualties—probably, if not certainly. *Wait, could it have been the guys of the 160th Chinook that we'd done a photo shoot with only a few weeks before? Naw, couldn't be.* It was daytime, so it was probably a conventional unit helicopter. Not that that was much of a consolation, but it distanced me from the fear. If it wasn't a 160th bird, then it couldn't be too close to home. At least that's what I kept telling myself.

"Hey, guys, need to get into the hooch!" I said to my fellow squad privates. "Jones said something about a bird down. We're being spun up for Cee-Sar." CSAR, or Combat Search and Rescue, was the task of securing a downed aircraft, or searching for missing personnel.

We soon huddled in the small wooden rectangle box that our squad called home for the summer, its only redeeming value being air-conditioning. The fact that we had only a team leader in front of us couldn't be a good thing. That meant our squad leader, Staff Sergeant Masters, I presumed, was in a high-level briefing and we'd have to wait for him to get further details.

If my teammates looked calm, I sensed that was only clouding a tension vibrating through each of our guts. How can you not be amped to think you might finally get thrown into the thing you came for? War. Only a few days before we'd been watching episodes of *24*, the TV show in which Jack Bauer gets thrown into, and escapes from, one death-defying situation after another, all in pursuit of protecting America, of changing the world for the better in some small way. Was this a Jack Bauer moment? Would we be recovering a helicopter crash site as we had simulated only weeks prior to taking over CSAR for Afghanistan? Was it finally our time to fulfill our mission?

We'd taken the training seriously, but it seemed extraneous, like something we had to learn but nothing we'd actually use; after all, Rangers weren't conventionally a CSAR-type unit. We assisted in all types of missions, like the Swiss army knife of Special Operations, but this seemed like an unlikely skillset we'd actually employ.

I started organizing my equipment before heading out and grabbed extra batteries for my PVS-14 night-vision monocular, my rifle's Aimpoint and PEQ-4 laser/illuminator. When I shoved them in the cargo pocket on my right leg, they rubbed against a thigh that I'd recently bruised when ramming it into a piece of rebar during a room-clearing exercise a few days prior. It was just above my right knee. My bad knee. The knee that blew up during that pickup basketball game in high school. *That damn knee always reminded me that simple things can go terribly wrong.*

"Weapons clean?" asked SPC Sal.

"Yes, specialist," I said, thinking, *well of course, they're clean.* Were they somehow going to get mucked up between last night, when he last checked on us, and today? Then I realized I was "majoring in the minors," concerning myself with trivial stuff, perhaps in a subconscious attempt to deflect an uncomfortable truth: the unknown that was hammering at my castle gates like one of those battering rams in medieval battles.

Oh, shit—the hair was standing up on my forearms like a frickin' crew cut. *Was I nervous?* I looked down at my armpits. They were drenched. All I could do was sit there and think about the helicopter. *What would it look like?* Everyone was presumably okay—*right?* As rehearsed, we would provide aid to the wounded, blow up what was remaining of the helicopter, then bring our guys home. Simple. *Let's do this thing!*

Staff Sergeant Masters entered the small hooch in a flurry. We called him "Hollywood" and he looked the part. But he was all business. The door slammed shut. He looked pissed, taking an abnormally long pause before looking us each in the eyes.

"An MH-47 helicopter from the 160th was shot down."

My God, it *was* the 160th, the guys we'd trained with and had our photos taken with.

"Sixteen men were on board when they were attempting to be a reinforcement element, for a recon team of SEALs." My nerves wound tighter. "We're primary CSAR. Get your shit ready, because we are rolling out in ten. Pack light but prioritize ammo. It will be twelve hours in and out. All of 1st squad is going, but the platoon has to cut a lot of guys to keep weight down. We have an active strobe on the site, and command believes that it will be a fight when we get there. Don't forget the lessons learned from Roberts Ridge. This is oddly similar. Let's go."

The words that resonated with me were "active strobe." Either someone—or a few *someones*—had apparently survived and the strobe was being used to signal for a rescue, or the enemy had activated the strobe, and couldn't wait for us to show up so they could shoot us down, too.

The "active strobe" was a blinking, high-output infrared light that had been seen by an A-10 Thunderbolt II surface attack aircraft surveying the crash site. American forces also detected an intermittent emergency radio transmitter beacon hit nearby. Both indicated that an American or Americans *might* be alive, and on the run. But the intermittent nature of each, and the lack of other radio contact, also indicated that the insurgent attackers might have captured the SEALs' gear, including a strobe and a beacon. It could have been a trap set by Shah and his men to lure yet another American helicopter into an ambush. And, of course, I would be aboard that helicopter.

It sounded like an in-and-out mission. Twelve hours. No extra food; we were just taking protein bars. And some awful terrain. We didn't get much else as far as intelligence.

We'd all studied a similar scenario atop Takur Ghar in March 2002. Roberts Ridge. That incident, which included Rangers and SEALs, resulted in heavy fighting. When the quick reaction force arrived, they were met with heavy enemy resistance from hidden bunkers. In short, a group of Rangers in an MH-47 were attempting to aid a team of SEALs and flew directly into a firefight. Before they even left the helicopter's ramp, the men were taking fire. This event resulted in the awarding of the Medal of Honor to both Senior Chief Special Warfare Operator Britt Slabinski and Technical Sergeant John Chapman (posthumously). Three Army Rangers were killed: Cpl. Matthew A. Commons, Sgt. Bradley S. Crose, and Spc. Marc A. Anderson. PO1 Neil C. Roberts, SrA Jason D. Cunningham, and Sgt. Philip Svitak were also KIA. It was one of the most infamous Special Operations missions gone bad in our history.

So, for now, all we knew was a bird with sixteen guys had gone down and we were being sent for rescue or recovery. Here's what we only learned later, the stuff that was basically the gist for the movie *Lone Survivor*. Something called "Operation Red Wings" had begun late the night of June 27, 2005. It was to involve surveilling and locating a Bin Laden wannabe, Ahmad Shah, and his IED factories in the region. Because Shah was a low-tier target, Special Forces would not allow its assets to be involved beyond the experts of the 160th Special Operations Aviation Regiment (SOAR).

The mission was a combined task force of Marines, Navy SEALs, and 160th SOAR personnel. The commanders knew they needed the cover of night to make this mission work. As with all night missions in a war zone, this one required a unique skill set. From the aviation side, 160th SOAR was the absolute cream of the crop when it came to nighttime flying. Forced by Special Operations doctrine of the time, protocol was to use a Special Operations Unit in order to gain access to the 160th SOAR. The operation commanders chose Navy SEALs because of recent successes in the region and the ability to work with Naval Special Warfare.

Four SEALs were to have conducted the reconnaissance portion of Operation Red Wings, locating and "marking" Shah's IED factories in the region. At least, that's what we were told at the time. Satellites and drones had already identified the factories; we needed "eyes-on" for confirmation, so we could blow them to bits with certainty.

Michael Murphy, Danny Dietz, Matthew Axelson, and Marcus Luttrell were the four SEALs chosen. While command didn't originally plan on placing such a small reconnaissance team so close to the target area without a Marine infantry unit as support, it ultimately did just that. Why, I don't know. As I too often said about life in the military; *it is what it is.* And SEALs don't tend to be guys who question a decision or back down from a challenge; this mission would be no exception.

The foursome had been tasked with gathering intel on a group of local Anti-Coalition Militia (ACM), led by Shah. The team ran into trouble soon after boots on the ground. Goat herders spotted them on the tree-studded slopes of Sawtalo Sar; the foursome had been "soft-compromised." What followed was far worse: a group of ACM (Anti-Coalition Militia), led by Shah, ambushed the four SEALs. As they scrambled down the mountain, trying to hold off the pursuit of nearly a dozen enemy combatants, three of the four were killed. Only Luttrell had survived—again, not that we knew this at the time. We had no idea whether the four were dead or alive.

A quick reaction force (QRF) of eight SEAL Team 10 members and eight members of the 160th SOAR was dispatched to extract and assist the recon team. Sixteen guys on a helicopter arriving to save four. And, *kaboom,* it had been shot down on the mountainside, right near the Afghanistan-Pakistan border.

MASTERS LOOKED AT JONES AND LUCAS. "WE'RE GOING to be walking a lot. Check your boots. Wear Danners or Oakleys. The terrain is bad so lighten up on everything except ammo."

Everywhere, guys hustled for their gear; the shot-clock was running down; I've never felt such a sense of urgency to get ready for something. CamelBak. *Check.* Boots. *Check.* Weapon. *Check.* Grenades times two. *Check.*

I turned my attention to the Skedco, a foldable litter that I was responsible for packing. My hope was that it would remain on my back and never be used. A classic item for the "new guy" to carry, it was rolled up like a cylinder and was in a bulky backpack that ran from the back of my head down to my mid-butt. Among the accessories? A body bag. In case I wasn't appreciating the gravity of this operation, the realization toggled me to full understanding.

SITREP: 4 hours since the crash of *Turbine 33*
Bagram Airfield

WE ARRIVED AT THE AIRFIELD AS THE MH-47S WERE warming up. The blades *thwack-thwack-thwacked* in the air of one of the "flying bananas" that dated back to the Vietnam War. Under night vision, the glow of the dual rotor blades was spectacular in infrared. The static electricity from the blades left two circular green glowing light shows. Like a laser at a night club, but without the drunken idiots. Just warriors. Warriors getting ready to do battle with an enemy that had just put a chink—a huge chink—in our armor.

I sat down with the Skedco on my back, using it as my own personal seat back. The only perk I had. As I stared at the glowing blades, I started to mentally prepare myself for what we may be getting into. The bird lifted off. I bowed my head, less in prayer than thought.

'Merica! We are coming for you, brothers.

My squad after conducting training on room clearing, complete with a shiner. (Courtesy of Felipe Peters)

Teammate and I heading out for some East River Range training near Bagram. (Courtesy of the Madslashers)

A joint 1st and 2nd squad training on Bagram. You know it was serious, because Doc Eddy joined us to make sure we were "taking our MF'ing Doxy" to prevent malaria. (Courtesy of Felipe Peters)

My full squad of C-1-1, the Pagans, at a night range session at East River Range. (Courtesy of Felipe Peters)

Russell, Todd, and I messing around after a vehicle-mounted, live-fire exercise outside of Bagram Airfield. (Courtesy of the Madslashers)

A photo that has been seen on message boards all over the internet with our faces blacked out. To correct all of the rumors and false claims, this is C-1-1 of 2nd Ranger Battalion outside of Bagram. (Courtesy of the Madslashers)

Vehicle interdiction training with the 160th SOAR outside of Bagram. (Courtesy of Felipe Peters)

More training with the 160th SOAR outside of Bagram. I can still feel the slap of dry earth on my face. (Courtesy of the Madslashers)

Lt. Jimmy Howell and SFC Congdon with a 160th SOAR M134 minigun over watching. (Courtesy of Felipe Peters)

SSG Masters and SFC Congdon after training with the 160th on Bagram. Turbine 33 in the background. (Courtesy of Felipe Peters)

My best friend and roommate, Hatfield, and I under a 160th SOAR M134 minigun mounted on an MH-47. (Courtesy of Justin Hatfield)

This photo was taken weeks before Operation Red Wings II. C-1 Madslashers, the primary Combat Search and Rescue element with an MH-47 of the 160th SOAR to our rear. Unable to confirm if this was in fact Turbine 33, Evil Empire. (Courtesy of the Madslashers)

6

SAWTALO SAR

OUR GUYS WANTED ON THE SCENE, LIKE, *YESTERDAY*.
We'd heard enough to suggest that our response could have been much faster. The helicopter had crashed at 1153Z. Now it was nine hours later, we were just en route, and we had 100 miles and some weather between us, at Bagram Airbase, to Sawtalo Sar to the east.

"Fucking officers are scared to lose another bird!" one guy grumbled. "For *fuck's sake*, we have an active strobe on the crash site!"

Another guy concurred with similar language, suggesting that this wasn't a Supreme Court hearing—or Mass. But, hell, we were frustrated.

"This is fucked! We should be on site—*slaying right now!*" he said.

On that first attempt to get onto Sawtalo Sar, so much adrenaline flowed through my body that I never noticed the temperature at Bagram—even at night it hovered in the mid-90s. But once we gained altitude and approached the mountain, the air grew bitingly cold and damp. We flew into the dense visual soup of a dying thunderstorm. Looking out from the helicopter, we saw nothing but darkness flashed with intermittent bolts of lightning.

The atmosphere was eerie. Like we were confident but realized this wasn't training anymore. This wasn't a video game. This was the real thing. Hardly anyone said a word. It's not in a Ranger's repertoire to say so, but I'll just say it: we were nervous. Wait. *I* was nervous. I just need to speak for myself.

I kept imagining what the first steps onto the mountain would be like. I didn't feel fear—I instinctively kept it from creeping into my psyche simply by looking to my left and then to my right, at my fellow Rangers. I looked to Lucas, my team leader. He was as cool as the Seahawks' Russell Wilson in the face of a safety blitz. Masters, a prototypical Ranger, was as ready as ever. His face said it all. No emotion. Just pure determination.

Next to him was Sergeant First Class Congdon. A beast. He towered over 95% of all Rangers and was as tactically sound as any of them. He could be as focused as a brain surgeon, except his job was exploding brains instead of fixing them. Not only was he big in stature, but also in personality. At times, he could be the kindest person on the planet, at other times Freddy Krueger in camo. A guy who ran toward gun fire when it erupted. A guy who I wanted on my side during any fight. He had the respect of every man in the unit. Hell, he was known throughout all of 2nd Ranger Battalion. He was the Led Zeppelin of Rangering.

A platoon sergeant in the Army is known as "Platoon Daddy." Even though this term wasn't common among the 75th Ranger Regiment, it fit perfectly, not so much because he was a father figure but because he was a mentor. He was a father of war and would lead us to victory. Any young private like me would be idiotic not to follow his lead. And every man in our platoon would willingly and selflessly follow him into any situation he took us.

Two people in front of me was my team leader, Lucas, one of the nicest guys I have ever met. A Texan, a Californian, hell, I didn't know. I did know that they raise them differently in Texas, and I for one seemed to get along with everyone from that great state. He was always clear on what his expectations were for any given task, always wanting us on the same page. Whether it was our group expectations or my personal expectations, he would make me confirm his orders before he moved on to his next task. I appreciated his clarity in leadership.

A few people behind me was Hatfield, my absolute best friend in the entire world and my roommate from Fort Lewis. Like me, he was from California, specifically San Jose. He was exactly what you'd expect of a Hatfield. Proud, fiery, and a joker, yet loyal as all get-out. An extremely genuine man with the utmost integrity. At Lewis, we'd done about everything together. Worked all day, ate some food, and partied all night—sometimes literally. We always had each other's backs.

Next to Hatfield was Russell, our resident Hawaiian, from Washington, although via Georgia Tech University. (It's a long story.) I don't think I ever saw him worry about anything. He was just like me: a good student who went away to college and ended up finding that it wasn't his time yet. He just did his job and did it well. No one ever had to worry about him doing anything wrong because he was a genuinely rock-solid Ranger private.

To my direct front was Sal. We called him "Slayer" or "Specialist Sal" when we were being "official." He was a true Midwesterner whose freckles and red hair belied his toughness. He was kind, but not weak. Oklahoma Sooner born and bred. One of the kindest souls to ever have the day job of a trained killer. He was always looking for the opportunity to play a joke or tease one of his brothers, a true joy to be around. This, despite being a "Tabbed Spec-4," a first-line leader in the 75th Ranger Regiment. A Tabbed Spec-4 may not get the glory of a non-commissioned officer, but he packed a punch.

As a Tabbed Spec-4, Sal's job was that of a disciplinarian for the squad, keeping in mind that everyone in the 75th Ranger Regiment above the pay grade of E-4 had already attended Ranger School, the top leadership course in the US Army. He didn't have to worry about losing any rank for "going too far" with a punishment on a private. Needless to say, you always treaded lightly, always respected the "Spec-4 Mafia." Sal would always be one of the first to offer assistance or lay down the hammer before a team leader had to intervene.

I saw the outline of Jones, another team leader in my squad, a little further back behind our group. He looked like he was asleep sitting up, but I couldn't be certain. He was yet another California Ranger from "the OC," the prototypical SoCal kid. He had tattoo sleeves, tan skin, and the flames of Hephaestus, the Greek god of forge and fire, in his soul. This guy was the most bipolar person I'd ever met. I say that in the nicest way possible because I loved the guy. One minute, he was your best friend, and the next he was ripping you a new one—that third point of contact, that is, when a paratrooper lands.

Sitting back a bit further was Larson. Specialist Larson was a quiet guy. Mostly kept to himself. He resided from Washington State, and his pasty white skin told that story loud and clear.

While I got along with him well, many in my squad didn't exactly pick him out as one of their favorites. After all, he did have a mean streak in him. Or should I say a streak of *I want to crush privates.*

Behind our squad was our attached Mk 48 machine gun team of Corporal Torres and Private First Class Sager. They were like our own personal guardian angels. When you have a machine gun team as effective as they were, you can't help but feel a sense of safety, like you're in your own personal safety bubble.

Torres, "Corporal T," hailed from Texas and was a Grade-A Badass. He was an excellent gun team leader and an even better dude. And he could let you know in his passive-aggressive and cerebral way of speaking. He would probably compare you to a character in history that you should know but don't, making you feel uneasy. I always enjoyed his wit and humor. He was as hard working as could be. If you needed a helping hand, Corporal T would be there. He would also crush you if you did something stupid, so there was that.

Sager, our assistant Mk 48 gunner, was one of the senior privates in our platoon. He was on his second combat tour as a private and was one of the next in line to head off to Ranger School when we returned from deployment. He was one of the smarter guys in our platoon and was well respected because of that. As a private myself, I relied heavily on the other privates for guidance. Their higher degree of institutional knowledge was invaluable. Sager was that guy for many of us. If you didn't want to feel the wrath of a Tabbed Spec-4 or your team leader, you'd ask Sager first. He probably had the answer. Sager entered the Army with dual citizenship in the United States and Canada. Upon applying for his secret clearance, he was asked to resign his Canadian citizenship. He did it—like he was supposed to— unlike another joker in our platoon who will not be named.

Last, but certainly not the least of my squad members, was our squad leader, Staff Sergeant Masters. He hailed from Arizona, where I spent my first year in college (University of Arizona). I didn't hold it against him, but he was more of a Sun Devils fan. Masters was a great Ranger. He always had his gear and body in tip-top shape, setting an example for all of us to follow. He was a big guy and extremely strong but was a surprisingly good runner. He would make us all hurt on Monday mornings because we would spend the weekends drinking the nights away and he would spend them with his wife and kids. A family man who would make us regret every weekend at Cowgirls Inc. He was mostly calm and collected and rarely had to lead with an iron fist, choosing instead to delegate that task to his team leaders.

Although he was only a few years older than his privates, Masters had years of experience at 2nd Ranger Battalion. This gave even the youngest of leaders an "old soul" feel to them. Masters was an expert at his craft and was an excellent teacher to boot. He would work diligently with all levels of his squad to ensure lethality during our train-up to this very moment. We were one great team, led by one great leader.

And where did Tony Brooks fit into the mix?

Good question. I think I was well-liked, partly because I never had a need to prove that I was better than anyone else; partly because I think the others sensed I loved belonging to this group; and partly because I did my job to uphold the goals of the team. I wasn't one of the strongest or largest, but I was a thinker, a problem solver. And—this might sound weird—I was probably the most "civilian" soldier of the bunch. The one that if thrown back on the street, would be the least likely to be picked out of a crowd as a Special Operations soldier.

By that I mean I embraced being a Ranger, but I never wanted it alone to define me. For some guys, I think, this was *it:*

the best they could ever be. And while there is absolutely nothing wrong with that because Rangers are elite, I never felt that way. I felt it was important, terribly important. But it was simply another life step for me, a chance for me to learn and grow and take those lessons into family and business and other avenues. I don't say that to assert any sense of superiority, but to simply point out that I was a different breed.

What I liked about it was being part of a team. I believe that when people come together with a common goal, the sky is the limit. You can accomplish almost anything. In that respect, if you were looking for a metaphor to describe my role on this team, I'd choose *glue*. Even as a kid, I was always able to see "the big picture," to put things in perspective, to see beyond what was happening in the moment. (Perhaps that's why my grandfather's death hurt so much, because I saw what a great influence he'd been on all of us and I realized that was now gone.) Regarding my Ranger unit, I would do whatever I had to keep the team unity intact. Sometimes that meant offering some humor, which came pretty naturally to me. And once it meant popping that guy in the face: because he was threatening our working together—and that not only wasn't right, it was dangerous. It could get people killed. Years later, when asked to describe me in a word, Hatfield would give me the ultimate compliment. "Loyal," he said.

RED WINGS II, A RESCUE/RECOVERY OPERATION, HAD begun. In the cockpit, the pilots could only see the glow of engines of other MH-47s around them through their night-vision goggles. And that glow dimmed as we flew further into the cloud. We had been flying for what seemed like forever. *Shouldn't we be there by now?* The air was getting much colder, the visibility poor because of a blindfold of thick clouds.

Then the call came; we were breaking off. *Shit!* Mission aborted. It was simply too dangerous. The incredibly well-trained and combat-honed Night Stalker pilots broke formation and climbed each MH-47 safely higher and away from the other birds.

I felt incredibly let down, confused, then plain angry. We were so close. And now we were turning around. *If we'd inserted, could we possibly have saved any of the SEALs or Night Stalkers? Were any still alive?* We all sat stone faced. I felt my jaw clenching. My head fell to a dead hang. *But, what about our guys?*

As we sped away from Sawtalo Sar, my gut sank and I felt breathless at the thoughts of the wives, children, mothers, fathers, fellow war fighters, and friends of those on the mountain—SEALs and Night Stalkers that might possibly have been saved by us, but who might have been left to die at the hands of another enemy, the weather. These were the rare situations that no manual, course, or movie could have prepared us for. I let out as deep a breath as I could muster as I looked left, then right. Never was the unknown more hellish than at that moment, having to leave our own.

SITREP: 30 hours since the crash of *Turbine 33*
Jalalabad Airfield. Insertion attempt number two

THE NIGHT STALKER MH-47S WERE PREPPING FOR takeoff. We were headed back. The second time had to be the charm, because our guys were beyond frustrated. To wait three months for the chance to do battle, then have your initial mission quashed, had us all gnarled in frustration.

The plan was for us to do a "fast rope" insertion at night from hovering MH-47s onto a small clearing as near to the crash site as was practical to avoid losing another aircraft. Once on the ground, we'd secure the site of the *Turbine 33* crash, search for any survivors, and then undertake the grimmest of all tasks, recovering bodies of fallen American service members and—if we were fortunate—aid any survivors.

"Don't forget to be on the lookout for hidden bunkers and fighting positions when we hit the ground," said Staff Sergeant Masters. "Most of these are tough to see from the air."

"Roger, sergeant," said a team leader. "Are we going to have air assets when we get there?"

"We are going to have multiple air assets—*weather dependent. We are ready to bring it.*"

I quickly loaded into one the five remaining MH-47s. I'd heard that the pilots and crew of another MH-47 accompanying *Turbine 33* when it was shot down were also part of the massive five-ship assault. These men had witnessed the crash and fireball.

The Night Stalkers, like my fellow Rangers, were incredibly tight with one another. They were friends in combat and back home. Their families knew each other. Their children played together. They hit the bars together when they were not working. I could only imagine what must have been going through their heads as all five MH-47s idled on the fringe of the air strip with a *thwack-thwack-thwack* of the burly rotor blades.

Although they'd seen the plume of fire and smoke and lost all radio contact with those of *Turbine 33*, I knew they'd held out hope. It is ingrained in all special operators to hold out hope for the best, but to prepare for the worst. We wouldn't have rushed to the crash site if all hope was lost. Maybe they'd all somehow survived. It would be our job to find out.

Our leaders weren't oozing with hope. "This will likely be a recovery mission, given the circumstances," said Masters. "The weather is awful. We are delayed getting to them. And the lack of radio chatter since the downing of the bird doesn't bode well for any rescue. We will be looking for tail number 146."

If some of the men had miraculously survived, time was not on their side—or ours. We needed to reach them ASAP.

I hated the sense that the enemy had drawn first blood. Hated it. I was, by nature, competitive; how many batting helmets had I cracked slamming them to the ground when I struck out playing baseball as a kid? Now, in the military, we always won, my team. *Always.* We were as ready as you can be for a situation whose particulars were as foggy as the weather we'd run into on our first attempt to Sawtalo Sar. It was one thing to visualize what it would be like to fight for your life, and vastly different, I imagined, to actually do it. I'd been visualizing our first fire fight since my time at basic training. Each time, I saw us winning. There was simply no other acceptable outcome.

I mean, you made the damn layup, right? Even if you wound up in the hospital in the process.

THE HELICOPTER TOOK OFF. I WAS CARRYING MY M4 with eight magazines, my 1.5 liter CamelBak, two bags of IV fluid, and the Skedco litter that I had previously stuffed with two body bags. We were told that the mission would take twelve hours—tops—so I brought no food.

As we screamed through the sky, I again thought about the families of those on the mountain and the notifications that would be sent back home to them. I hoped the notification went something like this: "A Chinook helicopter was shot down with sixteen men on board, *but* they are all alive . . ." I kept repeating it in my head. If I can only give those families some solace with that "*but.*"

I had a good view down the ramp and focused on the rope we'd use to descend onto the mountain. It was a much longer rope than I had ever seen (or even knew would be used for fast roping), about 100 feet in length.

The MH-47 sped toward Sawtalo Sar, hugging the terrain closely to mask for sound and allow less time for an enemy on the ground to respond. However, with that mapping of the earth came a lot of danger; after all, this wasn't a Hawaiian helicopter tour. I trusted the pilots one hundred percent, knowing that every jab and turn was carefully controlled—and for explicit reasons. From the outside, I suppose, the helicopter might have looked as if it were traveling as smoothly as a bullet train. Inside it felt like a dumbed-down roller-coaster ride.

Suddenly I saw the hand signal: an open hand with all five fingers extended. Five minutes to drop. In 300 seconds, we'd be sliding down the fast rope onto Sawtalo Sar.

Four minutes. . . Three minutes. . . Two. . . One.

I eyed my team leader and gave a quick head nod, the look on my face saying the words he'd never be able to hear even if I spoke them: "Let's do this!" He returned the nod, affirming my conviction in spades.

Thirty seconds.

I watched Congdon moving from rear window to rear window, trying to see the terrain and possible enemy below, underscoring the new sense of urgency I was feeling. The bird flared, forcing the rear sharply downward and the nose to the sky to stop all forward motion. I unclipped my safety line that was attached to the floor.

It was time. Looking out of the rear open ramp of the MH-47, I could see nothing but low fog and cloud cover. Darkness obscured the tall trees we'd been briefed about. With my PVS-14 night-vision monocular flipped up, I could only see a few feet in front of me.

The Night Stalker crew deployed the rope. My squad leader, our leadoff man, looked down, searching for green "chem lights," indicating the end of the line. He looked back and shook his head sideways, not a standard signal. He couldn't see the lights at all; the fog was too dense. But despite being unable to confirm that the rope was, indeed, on the ground, he went anyway. The second Ranger grabbed the rope and slid down, then the third, and the fourth. I was fifth man down.

The sky was a sea of nothingness, an amorphous swath of fog. I was sliding into the incredible unknown. With a death grip on the rope, I began my descent. The weight of my gear—about sixty pounds—burned into my shoulders, arms, and thighs. I slid down a foot, then five, ten, twenty, at which point it seemed as if a blanket were thrown over my head. I was deep inside the fog bank, at tree top level—no light whatsoever. My hands burned from the rope, the heat of friction toasting my leather gloves. Ten more feet, then another ten, then another.

For a moment I was suspended in both time and place, as if no earth or sky existed. Nothing. Just me and my fellow Rangers alone in the inky darkness.

How much farther?

7

BREAKING BUSH

SITREP: 32 hours since the crash of *Turbine 33*
3.5 miles SSW of crash site

I PEERED INTO THE FOGGY SOUP OVER MY RIGHT shoulder, sliding down toward what I hoped would be the ground. At the bottom of the rope, although not yet visible, should have been the faint glow of the green chem-light. Above me: the *thwack, thwack, thwack* of the helicopter. Down I slid. And slid. And slid. Was there no bottom to this black well?

I looked left, over my shoulder, hoping to see some vestige of that elusive chem-light stick below. Vaguely, as if dark browns and greens from an Impressionist painting, I saw something: rock, dirt, trees. I let go. *Aaaargggggghh.* It wasn't a scream; that would have signaled to the enemy. Just a grunt, only giving up sound I couldn't help but yield. Up here on this mountain, in these circumstances, quiet mattered. It might be the difference between life and death. Afghanistan met me with a large smack.

I bent awkwardly over something on the ground. No pain. Just the shock of being slapped by—a hard-rock planet. I instinctively rolled to my right side. Turns out, I'd fast-roped onto the top of some downed trees. (Yes, the Afghans log, too.) Wedged in the branches, I struggled to push myself up and get out of the way, lest the next Ranger in line plant a boot on my face.

One by one, more of the approximately twenty-five Rangers burned down the rope and slammed to the ground. *Bam! Bam! Bam!* Meanwhile, I wriggled like a crab on its back, struggling to get some leverage. I heard someone touch down within a foot of me; in my personal chaos, I couldn't tell who. I flipped my PVS-14 night-vision monocular down. As I started to get up, someone yanked me to my feet. Hard. It was a violent yank. Boom, I was suddenly standing up.

A senior Ranger scurried to and fro, clearing the landing area. Meanwhile, more Rangers slammed to the earth. I took a knee and gazed into the green hue of my night-vision monocular. Through an endless sea of fog, I could barely make out what appeared to be a valley. To my right: a sharp dropoff. To my left: a gradual slope up. Despite the racket, it was oddly peaceful. For now.

I swiveled my head back to the mountain where I could see only about 100 feet in front of me. My mind was on high alert, my eyes moving from tree to tree, scanning, searching, waiting for that enemy to show his face. Any moment an RPG or RPK could rain down on me. I tucked behind a tree for cover.

Then I heard it—"*Awwwwwwwwww!!!!*" It was a shriek of pain that no one wants to hear in these circumstances. A primal yelp that sounded like an animal in distress. A few moments later, Lucas tapped me on the helmet.

"Got an injury," he whispered. "Burt broke his arm on the rope-in. He's going to go ahead and walk into the crash site—no medevac."

I nodded. Burt was not just another Ranger. He was our radio operator. No wonder he broke his friggin' arm! I'd come down that rope like a runaway elevator, and he'd done the same, only with at least fifty pounds of extra radio equipment. But, it turned out, that's not what hurt him. What hurt him was another Ranger landing on top of him as he lay like a turtle on the ground with his radio.

Whoosh! The wind whipping up from the MH-47 increased tenfold as it popped up and away. I'd never seen a bird leave a scene as fast as that one. When the clouds and fog broke, you could see the spotlight of the moon, and it was as if the Chinook was bolting straight for it. I held my breath as they disappeared into the dark, unscathed. *Good. We already had one helicopter down; we didn't need another.* Once gone, I exhaled. *Success.*

My breathing was already coming hard. I expected the mountain's 9,364-foot elevation to play a part in this drama, but not the friggin' *lead role*. I hadn't walked ten feet before I was already laboring. There I was, on my first mission as a Ranger in Afghanistan, and I was already sucking eggs. Not how I pictured this going. Thankfully, I wasn't alone. I was surrounded by my brothers in arms. Brothers who had been tested over and over again to make it to this moment.

We were some four miles from the crash site, close enough to be there in a few hours, we thought; far enough away, we hoped, to avoid the enemy, which might be buzzing around the wreck like bees to honey. They might be stealing equipment, gathering intel, maybe even finishing off injured soldiers—or booby-trapping them for those who came to get them. *Us.*

"We're gonna be moving out in two minutes," said Lucas. "And we're gonna be moving fast."

I nodded.

He pointed to a small, muddy path at 11 o'clock.

"See that goat trail? We're going to take that as far as we can before hopping up to the ridgeline. Be alert. Watch my hand signals. This is prime ambush territory."

A second nod.

I scanned the horizon, looking and listening for any signs of movement. My breathing began to slow. I could still feel the warmth on my hands from the rope-in. No pain, so that didn't worry me, but I'd never had a lingering burn on my hands like this.

Then I reminded myself: *It's not about you, buddy, it's about them: the sixteen men who'd been on the chopper.* Congdon gave the hand signal; we were moving out. There was a gap about the length of a football field between One Charlie and Three Charlie, headquarters, and our PJ brethren. I watched as men seemed to appear out of nowhere from ahead. Rangers were scattered in the trees, hidden from view all along the goat trail. One by one, they moved out; I was toward the front of my platoon. About fifty feet between men. Just enough distance so you could still see the man in front of you, but not so much that you'd lose him in the fog or the dense tree line. It was a toss-up about which was thickest—the fog or the tension that shrouded the entire unit. Nobody spoke. All you could hear was the soft sound of boots at a steady pace. I placed my finger just above my trigger well on my M4, keeping the rifle low and ready.

Lucas, the man in front of me, turned to offer a "follow me" hand signal. I saw him disappear around a horseshoe bend to my 2 o'clock. While my instinct was to keep him in sight, I didn't want to move too fast because of the man behind me; we needed to keep some distance to keep a tactical advantage. Too close together and we were sitting ducks, too far apart and we'd lose communication and our combined fire power. With this being my first combat patrol, my only knowledge came from training and movies—mostly Vietnam movies. As we walked through the bush, I couldn't help but think of some of these classics like *Full Metal Jacket* and *Forrest Gump*. But those were fiction; this was real.

We'd been walking for only about forty minutes when I was jolted by the thought that I could no longer see Lucas. To my left was the goat trail and to my right a steep drop-off. I *could* see the man behind me and I signaled for him to keep pace. Now we hugged the terrain to the left as I walked faster. No time to waste. Finally, I spotted Lucas heading nearly straight up a rocky ridge like a mountain goat. *Oh, shit.* Lucas was on all fours, crawling like a bear.

As the fog gradually lifted, I could see more Rangers. Maybe ten. We were above the tree line. Now in the open, we were totally exposed to the enemy, if he was out there. It felt like back home, hiking in the Sierra Nevada and hearing thunderclap when you were above the timberline in late afternoon. The main difference? If lightning struck us now, it would be in the form of an ambush on the ground, not bolts from the sky.

Like Lucas, some of us had resorted to "four-on-the-floor" climbing. Hand and feet. Slipping. Sliding. Anything to get, and keep, a grip on the loose, rocky terrain. As I started up the mountainside, the weight of my gear—nearly two thirds of my body weight—wasn't doing me any favors. My feet slipped on the loose rock, though I caught myself. We continued straight up. Above me, I could hear Rangers doing the same. A grunt here. A quiet swear word there. From time to time, scree trickled off rocky nubs like waterfalls. This mountain had it all: jagged ridgelines, steep gullies, huge boulders. Everywhere loose rock, which, at times, made it like walking on marbles.

Each step and each finger grip were like grabbing a moving target; nothing seemed stable, including my confidence. My attention was no longer on being ambushed, but on falling down a mountain. I checked my watch. It had taken me fifteen minutes to move 100 feet. Take a step or two, slide down one. Take two more steps, slide down another. It was ridiculous terrain, like nothing I'd ever experienced.

On occasion, I'd hear some primal grunt of pain. Each time, it sounded like the same guy. Then I realized who: Burt. One-armed Burt. He was behind me, a few men back. Who could blame him? I could barely do it with two arms, and, with a compound fracture, he was doing it with one. The guy was a beast. He didn't complain once. *Buck up, Brooks.*

Thirty minutes had passed. I was still on all fours, crawling up this damn mountain. I looked up to see Todd, two to three guys ahead of me. His silhouette was undeniable. Big Todd slid down about forty feet. He looked like a cat that had all of its claws dug, taking chunks of the mountain as he slid. His slide sent rocks flying down the mountain. A few rocks shattered as they hit within feet of me, shards from it smacking the helmet and gear of the guy below me.

Suddenly, I slipped onto my right side and headed down the mountain. I tried digging my feet into the scree and took a small boulder to my right knee. "*Shhhhhhhit!*" I couldn't help but grunt as my thigh slammed into a football-shaped rock.

An hour into the climb, I could still see Ranger after Ranger below me falling and sliding all over the place. Drenched in sweat, I stopped and chugged some water. I looked behind me. The guys below, it appeared, had it worse than us—the more men above you, the more rocks heading your way. I crested the top of this rocky mess. My feet and knees ached with every step. My gear felt as if it had gained ten pounds, maybe twenty.

In Vietnam, American soldiers called the enemy in the night "ghosts." That's what it felt like we were looking for now. I had no idea if they were actually out there but sensed that they were. I waited patiently for movement or sound. In that moment, a sense of peacefulness washed over me as if the night were friend, not foe. It was the first of many times in Afghanistan when I would sense a security that I didn't feel during the day. Off base during the day, all bets were off; you felt exposed, naked, a target slapped on your back. At night, as a Ranger, you felt like the darkness—and the enemy—belonged to you. Part of it was the night vision, the sense that you had the eyes of some nocturnal animal that could see in a way others could not. Part of it was knowing our unit and air assets had forward-looking infrared devices and "thermal cameras" that could, if the enemy was out there, see men crouched in the brush, even if they thought they were well hidden. And part of it was simply knowing that we were Rangers and, like bats, did our best work at night. Whatever it was, in that moment I was soothed by a sense of peace that—

Whoo-whoo-whoo.

What the hell was that? Ahead, someone gave the hand signal for *halt.* Then I saw a hand to the ear. *Listen.* My heart rate shifted into overdrive. Sweat matted my face. The sound resembled an owl—maybe a sick owl. I repeated the signal with my left hand to my ear for the guy behind me. I waited for the sound again. My thumb was now resting on my rifle's safety. I knelt next to a tree, braced for what might be an impending attack. My weapon was at the "high ready" position.

I scanned the terrain below me to my right. I could see a small goat trail, and a canopy of trees. I looked with my non-night vision eye to see how bright it was. Now that the clouds and fog had lifted, the moon washed the mountainside in dim light—and increased the chances that we could be ambushed. We were, after all, near a location where a SEAL reconnaissance team just had been ambushed, and a helicopter had been shot out of the sky.

Whoo-whoo-whoo.

Again, my heart sped up. Ahead of me, Lucas stood up and sauntered toward me. He smiled.

"It was a fucking owl," he whispered.

8

BIRD DOWN
ON SAWTALO SAR: PART II

**SITREP: 36 hours since the crash of *Turbine 33*
300 meters from the crash site**

THE GLOW. IN THE DISTANCE, I SAW IT, THE UNQUES-
tionable remains of *Turbine 33*. We were almost there. We'd
sent up the Three-Charlie element to secure the perimeter. Just
short of the crash site, I saw a remnant on the ground: a piece
of metal, still smoldering. It didn't look real, but I knew it was
from the helicopter. Soon, at first light, we could see it: what
remained of the downed bird.

It was sad, pathetic, painful. What remained of me was no
different. Sick. Empty. Regretful. I was a hull of a man, a rifle
with no ammo . . . *Why these guys? Why not me?*

Up ahead, I could see part of the cockpit, and part of one of
the massive rotor blades. But mostly, all I could see was smoke
and scorched terrain. From my position, it was tough to get

a full view of what was ahead. I couldn't make out much of a helicopter. I was confused that a helicopter that was nearly two-thirds the length of a blue whale was able to hide on the side of a mountain. *My God, we'd just flown in on an MH-47 like this; how could it ever wind up crumpled and burned like what lay in front of us?*

I felt alone, a kid too far from home. Shouldn't I have been partying at the University of Arizona, where I'd be a senior? After all, it was summer break, wasn't it? But, no, not for the men of the 75th Ranger Regiment. Not today.

Now, in the Afghan morning, my hair was on end, my nerves frayed. Suddenly, something moved, back in the trees. I readied my rifle. Out walked two of our own, heading slowly toward my unit. PJs. Guys from Air Force Special Warfare, Pararescue specialists who'd been on the crash scene first. Obviously, they came bearing news. My stomach roiled. One of the PJs scanned us, looked down, then grimaced a tad.

"Nobody," he said, "is alive."

"Dammit," I said under my breath.

I hated that certainty. Hated that we didn't have a chance to help even one of these poor souls to get home alive. Hated that our enemy had prevailed. Hated losing.

Around me, some guys looked down, some looked to the sky, some looked around at others.

Our rescue mission had just become a recovery mission. Our primary task would be to find the remains of each man and safely get them home. First things first: find all sixteen.

Lucas, my team leader, walked over to me and Todd as we knelt. Todd was a fellow young Ranger, a fellow private in the 75th Ranger Regiment. This corn-fed, Eastern Washington boy was affectionately—and appropriately—nicknamed "Big Todd." He was one tough SOB and already had a deployment to Iraq under his belt. He was only about three to four inches taller than me but weighed at least forty pounds more. He could toss me out with the bath water.

"We're going to need all of the body bags," he said. "They're getting the rest of them up here. Get ready to move up—thirty feet or so from bird and stage to be briefed. Don't touch anything until we clear the area of enemy and possible traps."

In this part of the world, and with this enemy, you had to be on your toes. The Taliban was known to rig bodies of dead Americans with grenades, their pins pulled so that if the body were moved the grenade trigger would trip and the grenade would explode. They knew we'd come for our fallen brothers. And, yep, here we were.

We pushed down the side of the mountain to ensure that no enemy lay in wait, then headed back up toward the remnants of *Turbine 33*. There, we began setting up our pre-staging area. The tangled bird looked small, unimposing, beaten. All of which deepened my anger for the enemy that had done this.

I was on the far-left flank of the crash site as we cleared past it. We all gathered around, most of us standing, a few on one knee. The sun was just coming up, a touch of beautiful light meeting with the most gruesome scene I could ever imagine. A beauty-and-the-beast juxtaposition. My squad leader, Staff Sergeant Masters, approached.

"OK, guys, we have a perimeter set up by Three Charlie and the rest of One Charlie. First, we're going to drop everything and head down to clear the crash site. We're not sure if the enemy has been here and set up traps on the remnants of the bird or the bodies. Once we clear the site, we'll start to count the men and gather items for each guy."

Masters paused, breathed deep. "Then we'll get them into body bags and stage them over there." He pointed to a clearing, which was about the length of a football field—maybe two—from the crash site but about 100 feet above us, straight uphill.

Corporal Torres had a clear view of the valley below as he lay in the prone to our south, next to some large rocks. With an Mk 48, 7.62mm machine gun at his ready, he was our primary security element and, along with a few others, made me feel safe. We spread out. The search began. My mind was on two things: what I might find in front of me and what lay beyond. At any moment, the Taliban's AK-47s could begin to rain down hell on us. I was, I realized, spent. I was dazed from near dehydration, the altitude, the exertion, and the sight and smell of the wreckage. Beyond smoke, the overriding sensation was the scent of charred human flesh.

I scanned left, scanned right, wanting to find my brothers in arms and not wanting to find them. Wanting to believe that this was just some horrid nightmare and I'd awaken to find myself the old upbeat Forrest Gump I'd always been. From somewhere deep down, I felt the slightest instinct to flee: *Run, Forrest, run!* The quick answer: *Hell, no.* I was a Ranger. We ran *to* danger, not *from* it.

That's when I saw the first body: a fallen fellow US serviceman. A brother.

I knelt beside him. He was one of the SEALs, lying on his back. He had no visible injuries. None. Helmet on, weapon by his side with the selector switch on his rifle set to *FIRE*. He looked fine, as if he were only sleeping, at peace. He had his gear on as if ready for battle. He looked no different from guys to my right and left, the live guys, although he had a beard. *He was a warrior.*

As instructed, I looked for any sign that he'd been "disturbed"—i.e., booby-trapped—but couldn't find any. It appeared that all the pouches in his gear were full. I don't know why I felt comfortable doing this before we fully cleared his body, but for some reason I felt the need to connect to this hero who lay before me. Nobody was around. It was just me and him. I put my hand on his left shoulder, near a shoulder patch with a *31*, and looked him straight in the eyes.

"Sailor," I whispered to him under my breath, "you're going home."

IT WAS A SACRED TRADITION, THE IDEA THAT, IF humanly possible, nobody who was part of the US military would be left behind in any battle. Dead or alive. *You give your life for your country, we get you home.* The idea dated back to the Revolutionary War, meaning it was an American tradition that predated America itself. It survived the Civil War, when the Confederate army refused to return black Union soldiers it had captured. It played out in World War I and World War II, even after technology made it possible for a man to virtually disappear in the burst of a bomb. It continued to play out more than half a century after soldiers went missing in the jungles of Vietnam, on the shoulders of proud activists' ongoing searches for the remains of MIA or POW GIs who paid the ultimate price. And now, the tradition was continuing on a mountain in the nether regions of Afghanistan, a land so raw and remote that we might as well have been recovering bodies from the moon.

The Ranger creed, in the fifth stanza, said it bold and clear: "I will never leave a fallen comrade to fall into the hands of the enemy."

Why bother? some may ask. Because we owed it to the families back home. To the guy who'd given his all. To our brothers. And, I suppose, to ourselves. the effort symbolic of our all-for-one attitude that's as imprinted on a Ranger's psyche as if some sort of bar code on our souls that identified what—and who—we were.

The pragmatist/cynic might argue: *The guy's dead; what's the difference?* I'd argue that nothing could be more disrespectful than to leave a man who's already lost his life to then endure the shame of being alone in a foreign country. In such a case, nobody would ever know what a heroic human being he'd actually been. At the very least, the man's legacy should have a chance to live on. Thus, our desire to bring every warrior home.

As I knelt beside the first fallen soldier I encountered, I wondered whether he was single or married. Whether he had children. Where he hailed from. Why he'd enlisted. In the moment, I couldn't forget that I was soldier. But, beyond that, I was a human being. And, because of that, such thoughts were as invasive as the blackberry bushes back in the Pacific Northwest— prone to go wherever they damn well pleased, even places I didn't necessarily want them. If I'd landed on this forlorn mountain with killing on my mind, my purpose now had been redefined. My job was to find the dead and prepare them for their journeys home. Even if their deaths filled me with anger, my new-found purpose touched me with a sense of honor.

Until then, the worst moments in my life were ripping my knee apart and losing my grandfather. By most people's standards, I'd lived a pretty awesome life. No fault of my own, but I would venture to say that I was *not*, in that respect, the average Ranger. Many of my brothers had lived three lifetimes to my one. They'd had to fight for everything in their life. Overcome a helluva lot of obstacles just to be here. Me? I had two supportive parents; was, despite my hiccup as a freshman at Arizona, a model student; and, for the most part, had stayed out of trouble.

In other words, I didn't really deserve the honor that had been set before me. But perhaps because of that, I wasn't about to let anything distract me from taking this task as seriously as possible. As Todd and Jones joined me, I sensed that what was happening here was no less sacred than priests conducting Mass.

"Todd, I'll stand at his feet and you work his torso," I said.

As usual, Todd jumped right on the task. Sergeant Jones began to talk us through the next steps, making sure—for a second time—that the body hadn't been booby-trapped. Everything looked normal. Ammo undisturbed. Radio present. Gear still on him. Pouches on his tactical vest closed. I could see one grenade still tucked safely in his pouch. Everything checked out.

"OK, guys," said Jones. "Lay the body bag to the side. After you clear him, slide the open bag under him if you can. Brooks, cross his legs. Todd, you work the torso. I'll give you the 'all clear.' If it's anything else—be prepared to get the hell out of Dodge. Roll him back and get out of the way. Make sure you yell so everyone is warned. Got it?"

"Roger, Sar'nt," I said, almost in unison with Todd.

"Okay—on three—roll him. Wait for my clear, then give me a second to slide the bag over. Ready?"

Jones waited for us to acknowledge him, then said, "OK, here we go—one, two, three!"

Todd and I rolled our deceased brother to his side. I crossed his legs to get more leverage and Todd rolled his torso. We struggled to get him to his side, but after two to three yanks we heard Jones say, "Clear!"

We rolled the soldier onto a body bag. As we did so, a small object rolled to my left—something from the soldier's pack or pockets. I froze. So did the two others. It was a hand grenade.

"Oh, shit," said Jones.

Jones picked it up. Fortunately, it still had the spoon and pin intact. Good thing, because otherwise I'd probably have filled my britches—or been deader than the man I'd been helping.

Our taking care of this sailor was the first such ritual we would perform with others. But the hand grenade incident suggested a new method. First, we cleared each fallen warrior's grenades before placing the man inside a body bag. Genius, I know.

What struck me most about the helicopter victims was that most were not entangled in the wreckage itself. Most appeared to have either been thrown clear or had jumped from the helicopter as it careened toward earth. All were within about fifty meters of each other. A few were badly burned; most, frankly, showed little signs of trauma. I found this uncanny, given the force with which the helicopter had slammed into the mountain—and that the helicopter was either already on fire or caught fire on impact.

One of the PJs explained what he thought happened.

"It looks like these guys had unclipped their safety lines and were ready to rope when they were hit. The pattern in which they lay suggests they were thrown from the bird."

Hearing his theory, I felt like someone had kicked me in the gut. I had unclipped countless times from a bird, never imagining this as a possibility. Including the rope onto this mountain.

"A few of these 5.56 rounds have a firing pin mark on them," said the PJ. "These guys were returning fire."

In my head, I thought, *of course they were!* But I just stood in silence. I couldn't muster the courage to say a thing. I was empty. Once again, a sense of survivor's guilt: *Why them? Why not me?* For a moment I wished I could have switched places with them. They'd be looking down on me and bringing me home to my family. In a heartbeat, they'd have done the same job for me I was doing for them. No doubt in my mind. These men, even if I didn't know them, were giving others strength. Still fighting, despite being in Valhalla—that place in mythology where slain heroes are welcomed home.

Years later, some reports would say the Taliban had come across the crash and put two bullets in the head of all sixteen men. Absolutely false. None had bullet wounds. Not one. Most looked as peaceful as little boys sleeping in their beds back home.

We found our dead comrades fairly fast, most still wearing their rope gloves. My guess was that, as the PJ suggested, they'd been getting ready to rope when they got hit. We'd seen a rock outcropping that looked like the perfect perch from which the enemy could have fired an RPG.

Small fires from the crash crackled, nothing serious, nothing that was going to catch the forest on fire. Trees were smoldering, the earth was scorched. It might have initially been a pretty intense fire, but it was muted now. As for the helicopter, everything beyond the cockpit was MIA.

It seemed to us that the fire had prevented the enemy from grabbing equipment or booby-trapping bodies. We'd arrived more than thirty-six hours after the bird had gone down; by now the fire was only smoldering. But based on how blackened the forest was, it was clear this had been a serious blaze. Most of the SEALs were outside the fire zone. Some of the crew, however, hadn't avoided the flames; a few of the men were unrecognizable. Most of the dead were on their backs, lying flat, which suggested to me instant death; a few were in the fetal position which suggested otherwise.

At one point, we were trying to lift the pilots out of the cockpit, but it was hard. They kept falling apart. I reached for a man's torso, my arms under his armpits. I pulled—and got only one arm that had separated from the rest of the body. I couldn't help but feel bad for hurting one of my own. It might have been an irrational thought, but the pain was as real as slamming your finger in a door. And then someone pushing it shut to make sure it was closed.

IT WAS EERIE, BEING AT THE SITE. NOT ONLY WITH THE dead, but with the sense that we were being watched. The sense that the enemy was near. As the hours passed, the earth warmed, and I peeled down to an undershirt, my respect for the deceased only deepening. They had been tasked with reinforcing their brothers, the Navy SEAL reconnaissance team of Luttrell, Murphy, Dietz, and Axelson. And they had answered the call. They had sacrificed it all by jumping into the belly of the beast to help their brothers. That, in turn, meant families at home who would soon learn that they, too, were going to have to experience a heartrending sacrifice. Not just when they heard the news. But every day of their life. They'd never forget these guys. I knew I wouldn't—and I'd never met even one of them, other than training a few weeks prior.

I could not shake the thoughts of those families. As much as their families would love to have them home, I hoped they'd be proud to know that their sons and brothers and husbands went out on the most honorable terms. They went out while attempting to help other Americans in trouble. Who does that anymore these days—gives up their life for a stranger? They didn't sit back and do nothing. They were heroes. I would never forget them. In fact, I would later tattoo my left arm with a reminder of their sacrifice. I vowed to die with their memory in my soul.

Two hundred pounds of dead weight is not easily moved. It would take a few guys to get each body into a bag. Finished with that, we needed to move them into a clearing about two football fields away and multiple stories up the mountain—a clearing made possible by First Sergeant Garganta's explosives. We would stage them together and inventory all of their equipment. We needed to determine if the enemy was running around with sensitive devices that they could use against us—the same equipment that gave us a tactical advantage: radios, night vision, satellite phones, weapons, and such.

One by one, we carried the men up the mountain, where they would ultimately get a helicopter flight back to American territory. Each trip was a struggle. The smell was as wretched as a garbage can that had been baking in the sun. We slipped and fell, but, impossible as it might have seemed, we minimized the swearing. Every moment, at least in my mind, was sacred. Once on top of the ridge, as we inventoried, sweat dripped off my nose. By now the temperature was already nearing triple digits.

At one point, I had the briefest thought that I was doing some pretty heroic work. Then I looked at the guy next to me. There was something odd about how he was handling the bodies, as if nothing was going to keep him from helping but he wasn't physically able to give his all. Then I realized: it was Burt, the radio man who'd broken his arm on the rope drop. He was working with one arm, as if nothing had happened. *My God.* I was nothing compared to that dude. And I am almost certain that he was never recognized for his contributions, and he probably wanted it that way.

SITREP: 43 hours since the crash of *Turbine 33*
On the crash site

I LOOKED AT STAFF SERGEANT MASTERS, WHO WAS scanning something on a sheet of paper. He appeared confused.

"Sarn't, whatcha looking at?"

"Gotta problem, Brooks. Sixteen men on the list."

"And fifteen bodies found."

He nodded. "Take a look," he said as he handed me the paper and walked away. It was a manifest for this helicopter. I noted that three unit affiliations were present. The first eight men were from B/3 of the 160th SOAR, the next three from SEAL Delivery Vehicle Team 1, and the last five from SEAL Team 10. I read each and every name. As I slowly read them, I was simultaneously counting.

A. CW3 Corey J. Goodnature
B. CW4 Chris J. Scherkenbach
C. SGT Kip A. Jacoby
D. SFC Marcus V. Muralles
E. MSG James W. Ponder III
F. MAJ Stephen C. Reich
G. SSG Michael L. Russell
H. SSG Shamus O. Goare
I. SCPO Daniel R. Healy
J. SO2 Eric S. Patton
K. SO2 James E. Suh
L. LCDR Erik S. Kristensen
M. SO1 Jeffery A. Lucas
N. LT Michael M. McGreevy Jr.
O. HM1 Jeffrey S. Taylor
P. SOC Jacques J. Fontan

One man was still unaccounted for. I wasn't told who it was, other than it was a Night Stalker. A member of the helicopter crew. We shifted our focus. We needed to make sure we had sixteen men. If not, we were looking for someone who was out there being hunted by the enemy or, worse, *captured* by that enemy. We expanded our search area. I went further down the mountain with Todd, Sager, Salyer, Hatfield, and Russell. We pushed a reasonable distance down the mountain and—nothing. We spent an hour, possibly longer, searching every nook and cranny for the missing man. We were beyond exhausted. But we had to find the guy—that is, if he hadn't been captured or was miles away, trying to make it on his own. I remember reading a book, *Resolve,* about how some men in World War II in the Philippines had done that to evade the Bataan Death March—just taken off into the jungle and gone it alone. I wondered if there was one guy out there, doing the same; our 16th man was still unaccounted for.

As a math guy, what it all added up to me was disaster. Only later would we learn that the crash represented some sad military history: the greatest one-day loss of United States Special Operations Forces personnel in the history of Special Operations Command—as well as the single greatest loss of American troops, to date, in the American war in Afghanistan.

It was history that I wished had never happened.

Atop Sawtalo Sar, being briefed on the grueling task of crash site recovery. We were all gassed from the walk in, and the work had yet to begin.(Courtesy of the Madslashers)

Burned area of the *Turbine 33* crash. The bird sits directly to the left of this photo. The fog was moving out at this point. (Courtesy of the Madslashers)

Gendron, Pace, and Fortier inspecting the *Turbine 33* crash site days after the recovery. The somber faces reflect what we all felt. (Courtesy of the Madslashers)

9

SOLDIERS
AND THE SACRED

WITH EACH BROTHER WE PLACED INTO A BLACK, sterile-looking body bag, I felt a piece of me go with him. I don't say that with any false sense of drama. I say that because it's true. This was more than a "cleanup" operation. At least to me.

The experience is burned into my memory forever. Not only did I learn what war was on my first US Army Ranger mission, but I was "dipped" in it like some sort of baptism. And by dipped, I actually mean thrown into the deep end with my feet tied together. Not impossible to surface and swim, by any means, but not easy either.

The crash site was so horrific that we didn't need to destroy anything so the enemy wouldn't get it. Protocol was to destroy any remnants of the aircraft so that our enemies could not salvage or learn about its construction. The site of this crash had burned so hot and for so long that nothing recognizable remained other than one half of one rotor mast and pieces of rotor blades.

Meanwhile, I was deteriorating quickly with each drop of sweat, as if I were a melting stick of butter. My legs were still moving, one step in front of the other. Each weary step got shorter as the day went on. Each body we took up to the clearing was a little tougher than the last—emotionally and physically. We were slipping, falling, and scraping the rocky terrain as we maneuvered our way up. The "numbers" were taking their toll.

As we placed men into those black bags, things happened that still haunt me. Sometimes, there was no other way to get a body into the bag without breaking bones. I knew that the men were not alive, but the sounds made by breaking limbs don't change: like crunching tree limbs. Still, even if it was necessary, I didn't have to like it. And I didn't. Not at all.

And then there was the burned flesh. Skin is not meant to be burned. It loses its integrity. Out of respect for these men and their families, I will spare the detail, but you get the idea. It was about the most frightening scene imaginable, one that I remember as if etched into my memory with a hammer and chisel.

As I sat down on the charred remains of a tree, the smoke hung over the scene like a pall of death, assaulting the nose as much as the eyes. It was awful. And I was already a battered shell of a man. Despite being healthy, breathing, and relatively safe, I felt as if my heart had been ripped out of my chest.

Thump! We all jumped up and looked to our south. *Boom!* The sound of a rocket-propelled grenade shattered the quiet. *Crack-crack-crack-crack-crack-crack-crack-crack-crack.* An AK-47 was firing in the distance. We grabbed our gear. *Crack-crack-crack-crack-crack-crack-crack-crack-crack.* We took a knee, bracing for whatever might be coming our way.

The radio squawked. "We have eight to twelve enemy moving north towards our south-blocking position," a voice said.

"Get your shit ready to go," said Masters. "They're asking to get clearance for The Goose." How do you explain The Goose? Think of a bazooka, but modern-day and with rounds traveling at three times the speed. It is an 84mm recoilless rifle, fired from over the shoulder, that could reach out and rearrange an enemy's body parts from 1500 meters away.

Its official name was the Carl Gustaf, a monster of a weapon manned by Peters, who obviously was pumped to hear he might get a chance to fire the beast. Judging by the smirks on our faces, the rest of us were eager, too. When "The Goose" was on your side, it made a light infantry unit jump up to another level of lethality.

Then came the letdown. "The enemy are outside its effective range," said Masters, "so all Rangers are holding tight."

In war, you never want to reveal how much firepower you have unless you are certain that it is needed, or you're certain that no enemy is watching and gaining intelligence on your force. This time, The Goose was held back—a smart decision, I believed.

As we knelt at the crash site, Rangers to our south were showing incredible discipline by watching the enemy—and not engaging. Yet.

Thankfully, our guys knew the weapon systems better than the enemy. Sitting at the southernmost position of our security perimeter was our attached Air Force Joint Terminal Attack Controller (JTAC), "Sandy." He jumped on the radio to call for air assets in the area. Within ninety seconds of that first RPG air burst, "Sandy" had two A-10 "Hawgs" inbound. An A-10 is a single-seat jet designed to support ground troops with close air support. "Sandy" decided the best course of action was to fire

2.75-inch, 70mm rockets with flechette rounds—crazy, dart-like objects—toward the enemy. Within minutes the A-10s screamed overhead.

The rockets pounded the enemy incessantly. The sound of an A-10 firing rockets is hard to explain. Not only did I feel each and every launch but heard the glorious sound that followed. Afterward, all was calm, as if time had stopped. Hatfield was next to me, on a knee. He looked in my direction with a smile from ear to ear.

"Now that was as 'merica as it gets. That was fucking awesome."

All of us chuckled, knowing that our JTAC just took out a group of men coming to fight. As much as we all wanted to be in that fight, we would much rather win—and we would take it any way we could get it. No shame in winning the game in the first inning. We laughed—"would like to see The Goose get a shot at them," someone said—and returned to the task at hand.

How could we laugh, some might ask, while preparing sixteen soldiers in body bags? Because if we hadn't, we would have cried. If we hadn't leavened the experience with at least a touch of laughter and irreverence, we never could have gotten through it. And not once was any of our "healing humor" aimed disrespectfully at the dead; on the contrary, that part of the job had a sense of sacredness to it. And I can say without a doubt that had the tables been turned and it had been sixteen of them preparing sixteen of us, their attitude would have been exactly the same—deep respect for us with shallow dives into humor here and there to keep from going bat-shit crazy.

Think about even seeing a single person who's dead, perhaps an older person who keels over of a heart attack in a public park. It'd probably jolt you, wouldn't it? Now, consider sixteen people with their entire lives ahead of them, folks with whom you shared one of your life's deepest experiences. And consider that you hadn't just seen them lying there, but had to physically move them, one after another. All day long, up a mountain. In doing so, perhaps you can understand the emotional tightrope we were all walking; I can't answer for the others, but my equilibrium was as taut as a violin string.

SITREP: 44 hours since the crash of *Turbine 33*
On the crash site

AND WE STILL DID NOT HAVE THE SIXTEENTH MAN. After hours of searching, we were becoming increasingly frustrated. Our main objective was to find every American. And based on the scene, I doubted that someone could have survived two days after this horrific crash. Our platoon's leaders gathered just above us near the crash site. They were on the radio, discussing the next steps. We continued looking at the burning remnants of the Chinook. Using sticks and branches to sift through the rubble. Where was "Sixteen?"

Two new people joined the search: Lieutenant English and his radio operator, Recinos. It was like a breath of fresh air. I overheard Staff Sergeant Masters talking to Lieutenant English.

"Sir, we have pushed down this hill about 100 meters and walked on a line all the way back up. No sign of him anywhere."

"Keep looking. He's here. Has to be close."

There was something about the confidence English exuded that motivated men. Not only was he a former enlisted man, but also a former member of the most elite counter-terrorism unit on the planet. He was one of a few that I would consider to be "beyond human." A superhero in camo.

Recinos was below us, just below the cockpit of the downed bird. I could still see smoke from where he was crawling around

111

amid the hot embers and what was left of a tree. He saw something that, at first, looked like the limb of a tree, but then, he realized, was the limb of a man. Everything, tree and soldier, was burned.

"Got him!" he said.

Number Sixteen. Found. All the men aboard *Turbine 33* were now confirmed to have been killed in action. None had been captured. It was both a victory and a defeat. We now had accounted for our sixteen warriors. But our last hope that one might still be alive was gone.

For a kid who, twenty-four months earlier, had been partying and sleeping through college classes, this tsunami of death was forcing me to grow up in a hurry. Not, of course, that anyone else could know that. A soldier keeps his emotions in check—or as in check as possible. What I'd started to realize is that all the rules and regulations and training and protocol could certainly help you become a Ranger but couldn't stop you from being human. If Peguero's death had reminded me of my own vulnerability, the death of the sixteen on Sawtalo Sar reminded me of my country's vulnerability. As cocky as we Rangers could be, the reality was that war batted last.

It would only be years later that I found in this carnage a lesson I hoped to pass on to my own children: *never apologize for being human.* And never allow anyone to pound the humanity out of you.

After having seen the toll of death on that mountain, I, couldn't help but wonder if anyone back home would appreciate the sacrifice. Hell, would even *hear* about the sacrifice. Some, I suppose, would grieve. But many others, I figured, couldn't have cared less. They were preoccupied with their Myspace account, their latest Black Eyed Peas album, or some other triviality to care about someone else dying for their right to live free.

SOLDIERS AND THE SACRED

The wars in Iraq and Afghanistan hardly produced the all-in-this-together feel of World War II nor the rancor of Vietnam. Ours were the out-of-sight-out-of-mind wars. The general public didn't know war beyond a *Call of Duty* video game or the latest combat movie. When *Call of Duty 2* debuted in 2005, the year we arrived here, 250,000 copies sold in the first *week*. Meanwhile, an entire *year* of recruiting didn't produce that many new military officers. We weren't yesterday's news. We weren't news period, unless, of course, one of our helicopters went down. Then we were all over the headlines—for failing.

As I sat amid my first mission in a combat zone, I felt as if we'd done something important, but who really cared? It didn't matter. Nothing did. War, I'd quickly learned, was not, as I'd thought, glorious. War was ugly. Everyone lost something on that day. The soldiers and their families certainly did. America certainly did. And I did. I'd been baptized by fire, the smoke from that wreck casting my naivete of war into the Afghan skies.

Always the analytical one, I had learned back in training to imagine myself not as "man" but as "machine." Such thinking had helped me override the feeling of quitting. But my calculations hadn't considered days like this, the "feeling" stuff of my humanity that, I realized, could only be "willed away" to a point. The human spirit is stronger than any machine we can conjure ourselves to be, and I make no apology for that. Still, the two forces create an emotional struggle.

For years after the war, I considered the pain and frustration and sheer sadness I felt that day as something like a Scarlet Letter of shame, like they weren't "Ranger-worthy." But in time I would come to understand those feelings differently. I would come to see them as badges of courage. They reminded me I was human in the same way I was human when, at thirteen, my grandfather's death absolutely shattered me.

The pain of having to put sixteen bodies in bags tore me at my soul's deepest levels because I overlaid my love of my own family with what I assumed was the love each of the sixteen families represented on this mountain would feel when they got the news about their sons.

Each of those human beings, in some ways, was irreplaceable. Each would be missed by many. I knew that I'd miss them, and I didn't know them as much as I did a couple of clerks at my local supermarket. But those men and me—we had a common love. The love of country. The love of liberty. The love of being at the tip of the American spear. It didn't matter that I didn't know them. They were family. My extended military family. And they needed to go home.

I took a knee, bowed my head, and took one long, deep, burning breath.

10

A RING IS FOREVER

SITREP: 45 hours since the crash of *Turbine 33*
On the crash site

DURING A SHORT BREAK, TODD LOOKED AT ME WITH HIS normal puppy dog face. "What do you think happened?" he asked, nodding to the crumpled copter.

"No clue. Can't imagine that it was an RPG. It would have to be a perfect shot to do this—right?"

Todd nodded back. He should have just kicked me as hard as he could—directly in my gut. That would have been the best way to replicate the pain that consumed me.

"Maybe a stinger missile?" Hatfield chimed in.

We stared at the charred earth in front of us as if we'd just seen a ghost. No emotion, just empty stares. We all sat frozen in position, frozen in our thoughts.

Could it have been a weapon that our government supplied to the mujahideen a few decades prior? I didn't want to believe that. Not even a little. But the possibility certainly existed, based on what we could see on site. In 1979–80, under President Jimmy Carter, the CIA provided funding to the mujahideen in support of their war against the Soviet Union in Afghanistan. The policy continued under the Reagan Doctrine, stinger missiles delivered en mass to Afghanistan's mujahideen. As anti-aircraft rockets, stingers would have been perfect weapons to shoot down a US helicopter. And we knew that even though "most" stingers had been recovered from this era, some had not. Hundreds of them had not.

Either the enemy was hidden like a virtual ghost or he fired from a clearing and quickly retreated to the wood line. Either way, it had to have been a lucky shot—for him. At least that's what I wanted to believe. We knew the enemy was relentless, fought hard, and saw us as nothing more than faceless "infidels" to be stamped out like intruding ants. But it was also hard to cut the enemy even a sliver of respect, not when you remembered the loss from 9/11.

Amid the conversation, I heard that one of the dead had once been a Ranger, former Third Battalion guy.

"Hatty, hear that?"

"Hear what?"

"What Congdon just said. One of the guys was a former Third Batt guy. Muralles."

"Are you kidding me? This shit sucks. We gotta find the assholes who did this."

Up until this point, the sixteen hadn't seemed completely like "us." They were Navy, we were Army. They were SEALs and we were Rangers. Or they were aviators and we were not. Yes, they were also elite. Yes, they were also members of Special

Operations. Yes, they were fighting the same war. But they were not from our unit, and we had a degree of separation from them.

This was different. The scowls on our faces could have cleared a room. We looked at each other and shook our heads. *Was I in an alternate universe? How is any of this actually happening?* The loss now hit us right on the shoulder, where our unit patch would traditionally be on our uniform. That one simple fact put a new chink in our personal armor. It wasn't just "fellow Americans" anymore. Now, it was a fellow Ranger.

I began thinking about our own ride on an MH-47 just a few hours prior. *How hard would it have been to shoot us down?* By the looks of it, not that hard—and yet it was rare for something like this to happen.

I tried to imagine the horror that must have sliced through those on board with the suddenness of a stab from a sword. The jolt of panic. The flash of fear. The feeling of complete helplessness. I imagined the families getting the news—the worst-case scenario that every military family dreads on each and every deployment. The fear of losing a loved one. The fear that that last hug and kiss goodbye was indeed—*the last.*

Sergeant First Class Congdon walked over to our small huddle and began to update Staff Sergeant Masters.

"First sergeant is going to be working on this landing zone so that we can exfil these guys tonight. Let the guys know that we need all of their explosives. And listen—the 160th Commander, Commander Reich, was married a few months ago and we didn't find his wedding band. We need to get some guys over there and help look for it in the bird."

"Roger."

The challenge enlivened what was an otherwise tired bunch of soldiers. We quickly got onto our feet and headed toward the smoldering remains of tail number 146. We suddenly had a new purpose. Something that gave us an ounce of rocket fuel to move forward.

Part of it, I suppose, was the competitive nature of every Ranger I've ever known. Every guy there, I surmised, wanted to be the guy to find Commander Reich's ring. I know I did. And part of it was that in a sky full of the darkest clouds, even the slightest silver lining brings inspiration. To find that ring would be one small "feel-good" touch to an otherwise stomach-churning day. We weren't doing it for our unit, even for our country. We were doing it for the guy's spouse. It wasn't much—we'd much rather bring home the guy alive—but, for now, it was all we had.

I hopped around to the right side of the bird, slightly behind where the cockpit lay, my feet sinking slightly into the layer of ash and soft debris. I grabbed a small stick, about the size of a pencil, and while in a full primitive squat, began sifting through the ash. I was praying for a miracle. And thinking, oddly, about a certain bartender back in Seattle.

The beautiful dimples. The almond-shaped eyes. The kind disposition that seemed a tad out of place for a young woman serving drinks behind a bar. In short, the woman who, try as she might, could not say no to me.

When you're only twenty-two, you're not prone to think about marriage, picket fences, and a couple of smiling children. But I'd be lying if I hadn't tried on the thought of kissing that woman, of feeling her kiss me back, of maybe even her in a white dress and me slipping a ring on her—

"Brooks," said Hatfield. "You've got that 'Heidi' look in your eye. Don't let your mind wander, asshole. Find the damn ring!"

"I will before you will."

"Dig, Brooks, dig," said Hatfield.

I dug, dug, dug. I sifted, sifted, and sifted—until my back and legs began to cramp. I knew this feeling well. I immediately reached for my water, only to find that I was nearly empty. *Shit,* I thought as I finished the last few drops. My experience thus far in the military had taught me that staying hydrated could make or break you. Even the strongest of men could be crumpled into rubble without enough water. Ours was to have been a twelve-hour mission. By now we were already into "extra innings"—three hours' worth—and still had plenty of unfinished business. While I expected to soon be on another MH-47 headed back to Bagram, I couldn't help but feel a flash of panic when my last drop of water trickled down my gullet. My uniform was drenched in sweat. My legs and back ached. My feet had that "hot-spot" feeling suggesting flaming blisters were about to burst.

There were five of us within an arm's reach of each other, either down on all fours, on one knee, or in a primitive squat like I was. Nothing. Ten minutes of fruitless searching seemed like an hour. We were taking thirty-second rest breaks after each minute of sifting as we looked at each other, hoping and praying that someone would find the prize.

I looked to my brothers to my right and left for motivation. They all looked like they had been in a fight, but here they were, driving forward—not to thwart the enemy but to find a brother's ring. Not one complaint. Not one person feeling sorry for himself. Not one thinking this task was beneath him.

Me? The longer we looked, the more I saw this mission as a sliver of salvation, an honor, a duty. Had any one of them been the man who'd lost it, he'd have wanted the Rangers to do the same for him. I imagined the guy's young wife having that ring given to her. How much would it mean for her to hold it in her hand? How much might it help warm a heart chilled by death?

We had to find it. It wasn't an option to fail. Nothing mattered more in that moment than that symbolic and sentimental piece of jewelry.

Boom! Crack!

The noise shook us—a loud explosion about 100 meters to our west and slightly above us. The trees were crunching and falling from the explosion. A loud, jubilant yell rang out from near the explosion. First Sergeant Garganta, it turned out, was detonating explosives to clear out the helicopter landing zone. The entire valley heard what was going on. We were here to conduct business. Despite announcing our presence to everyone within twenty miles, we needed to make damn sure that we had a huge landing zone. He was making the job of landing an MH-47 a bit easier in this wild terrain landscape flush with evergreen trees. We were told that this detonation would be happening, but it still scared the shit out of most of us.

"Looks like we are going to have HLZ Gar-gan-taaa uuup in this bitch," Hatfield said in his best Ice Cube-ish voice. We all smiled as we looked over at the first sergeant having a literal blast while clearing trees for an eventual MH-47 landing.

I leaned over to Todd. "How are you on water?"

"Good—I think. I have a full bottle."

"Do you think I should open our spare bottles from the litter? I'm out."

"You carried it. If you're out, go for it."

I did. Meanwhile, the group of men surrounding the downed Chinook grew. There were no less than a dozen Army Rangers and two PJs crawling around on the ground, digging and sifting for a golden ring of hope.

As I moved toward the empty hulk of bird, my mind drifted to the reason we were all here in the first place. *Where in the hell were the four guys who these guys came to rescue? Could they be nearby? Are they on the run?* We hadn't heard any updates, so my assumption was that they were, indeed, on the run or that someone had already linked up with them. No news, I figured, was good news.

I resumed my search. This time, I moved a bit further behind the cockpit, still on the right-hand side. I grabbed a slightly bigger stick this time and began moving ashes with a light wiper-blade-style action. It was like trying to find a pea in the Pacific. I took a knee in the thick layer of ash. Nope, not there. I took a knee on a hot spot that quickly had me moving to my left. Nope, not there. An hour passed. Another. I'd covered an area only the size of small kitchen table and, for the first time, was starting to feel a sense of—

"Got it!" a Ranger yelled.

Whoops and hollers broke the silence. I jumped up with a fist flying in the air.

"Hell, yes! We got it! Great fucking job!" More cheers.

It was our first moment of victory since we'd arrived on the mountain. I'm not sure who found it, but high fives flew left and right as if we were kids who'd won the Little League World Series. Smiles abounded. Amid a bowl of shit soup, it was a moment of pure happiness.

We could give the man's wife an item that she absolutely deserved. An item that had meaning beyond anything I'd experienced in my life.

This ring could not be taken from her. Not here. Not now. Not ever.

11

DEATH WATCH

SITREP: 47 hours since the crash of *Turbine 33*
Helicopter Landing Zone (HLZ) Thresher

WE WERE GATHERED AT THE HELICOPTER LANDING ZONE that First Sergeant Garganta had spent the day clearing with his big-boy explosions. Nearby lay the black bags that we had carried up the side of the mountain. Our boys were going home tonight—God willing.

As I said, I'm not an overly religious person. Spiritual, yes, but I am not church-going spiritual. But you'd better believe I was asking a higher power to see these men back to their rightful place—with their families back home.

"Listen up," said Masters. "We're getting transponder hits in a neighboring valley, the Korangal Valley. We're linking up with SEAL Team 10 guys and heading down to see what it is. Might be the four SEALs from the reconnaissance team."

If the weariness of the day had dulled anyone's focus, this news sharpened us in a hurry. We looked in the eyes of our squad mates—all business.

"We don't know who is behind these transponder hits, so we need to be vigilant," Masters said. "It could be a trap. It could be the same guys who did this shit." He nodded at the smoldering remnants of *Turbine 33*. "Drop your plates, lighten your load if you can, and stay hydrated. We're probably going to be up here a while."

Like the others, I began removing my front body armor plate, stacking it with the pile that Masters and Jones had started. It probably weighed less than eight pounds but after wearing it for more than fifteen hours, it weighed on me as if one of those old deep-sea-diving suits. It felt fantastic—and oddly motivating—to get it off. As Rangers, we took the small victories and ran with them. But I couldn't get too hyped up; I still had to carry the damn emergency litter. A beautiful piece of equipment if you needed it. Hell to carry.

We were ready to roll within minutes.

It was late afternoon, June 30. As we waited to link with SEAL Team 10, most of us had been without sleep for twenty-four to forty-eight hours—and working on the side of a mountain for the past twelve. We were tired, hungry, and thirsty. But who needed sleep, food, and water when you had adrenaline? It had fueled us since our boots had hit the ground.

I've heard this before regarding athletics, and I think it's true about war: *As well trained as we were, when challenged in the actual "competition," we could do far more than we thought we could.* I attribute that to being part of a unit; studies have shown that men can withstand more pain when part of a group than by themselves. Whether that's due to machismo or the will to help "the village," I believe it. I think wanting to help another person—or worrying about *failing* to help that person—is a great motivator.

Most of us, I think, preferred a fight. I know I did. But the only wars that are non-stop fights are the ones in movies. The reality is, a lot of what soldiers do is train, wait, reposition, and carry out an array of other non-combat "action." Anyone who tells you otherwise, frankly, is full of shit—especially if the reference is to the Global War on Terror (GWOT).

Was there fighting in Afghanistan and Iraq? Of course, some of it intense and long-lasting. Were some areas experiencing more than others? Absolutely. But, in at least one respect, the GWOT was no different from any other war: We did a helluva lot of waiting. A lot of posturing. And a lot more waiting. Timing was everything. Especially if you wanted to do things right. If you wanted everyone to come home.

Ask the average American about war and the only thing they think about is combat. It's like the cop who shows up at career day at the local high school. What questions are they asked? *Have you ever killed anyone? What kind of gun do you carry? Can you tell us about your coolest shoot-out?* The reality is that cops rarely fire guns. And, outside of training, most military personnel rarely do either.

After World War II, military writer S.L.A. Marshall (*Men Against Fire*) famously asserted that no more than one-fifth of US infantry ever fired their weapons at the enemy in combat during the war. John Keegan, in his post-Vietnam book, *The Face of Battle,* put the number at twenty-five percent. Personally, I doubt the numbers are as low as either man suggested in infantry units. Still, basic empirical evidence suggests combat-to-non-combat time in war—even for those in combat units—was, and is, incredibly low.

Listen to the stories of men who fought in World War II's Battle of the Bulge and you'll learn that they spent a lot more time shivering in foxholes, probing the German line on patrol, and simply waiting for engagement than actually fighting. And fighting actually came more in short bursts than in prolonged battles.

All of which is to say that war is much more like baseball than football. The latter is wave after wave of action—more than 100 action-packed plays per game. But in a three-hour baseball game, only ten percent of it is comprised of actual "action," according to a 2013 *Wall Street Journal* study. In Afghanistan and Iraq, that's not far from the truth. Don't get me wrong; I'm not diluting the heroism that our soldiers have shown in the heat of combat. I'm simply saying that protecting our country's freedom by our presence in Afghanistan and Iraq has involved more than 2 million soldiers, the vast majority of whom never shot a bullet.

SEAL TEAM 10 SOON ROLLED IN WITH A PURPOSE. NOT only did these guys mean business, they *looked* business, their eyes chiseled in determination. Their very presence torqued our own resolve another notch or two. Half of the men on *Turbine 33* were from their team. Four of their own were out there some-where. Dead? Alive? Wounded? Who knew? But the transponder hits meant our mission was changing.

Many of the SEALs walked past us and headed for the black bags that hid their buddies. I felt their pain. And my uneasi-ness. Something didn't feel right. A couple of SEALs began to open the black bags. They would go from bag to bag as if they were searching for something—opening each and every one. In some ways, I felt as if they were undoing what we'd done, pawing through bodies that we'd already prepared for the trip home.

I felt a giant rope beginning to knot up in my stomach. And it wasn't just a matter of turf. They had every right to be doing what they were doing—these were *their* guys. Meanwhile, in our silence, each of us was left to interpret what was really happening here.

In my mind, this was no social call. They weren't out to pay their pals any final respects; that, I presume, each man had already done in his own way. Instead, they were going through pockets, looking for gear they could use—and, I suppose, a memento or two that they could help get back to their loved ones. Fulfilling the "if-something-happens-to-me" promise many of them made long before it had come to this.

I had a similar talk with a few of my buddies. One asked me to make sure his kids were taken care of. That was a tough one. I didn't think I had it in me to check in on kids that I'd never met. But I would make sure of it. Another asked me to do the unthinkable.

"Brooks, if I get shot in the dick, take me out," said a team leader as we were training just outside of Bagram Airfield in Afghanistan. "I can live without an arm or leg, but not my dick."

"Hell, you know I can't do that," I said, hoping he was only joking but knowing he probably wasn't.

Back on the mountain, watching the hasty searches unnerved me. Not that anyone was doing anything wrong. Whatever they were looking for, every soldier who dons a uniform knows that's it's just part of the deal. Whatever's best for the team, the squad, the country.

What started pinging my own emotional buttons was the obvious emotion these guys were feeling in the process. This was no looting spree, I began to realize. This was operators doing what operators had to do.

I watched as they knelt above each man. Most, of course, swallowed their grief deeply, not wanting to show any emotion to

127

their brothers in arms. A few couldn't do that. One guy covered his face and wept. Another walked away and stared in the sky, as if either beseeching help from On High or wondering how in the hell God could let good men die. And the toughest of all was the guy who just grabbed and hugged his fallen brother. Weeping and yelling "Why? Why?" while embracing him as if they had not seen each other in years. It tore me up inside. I tried to look away—I felt like a voyeur uninvited to this outpouring of emotions—but could not.

Nobody suggested stuff like this would happen in war. I felt like a food processor was whirring in my stomach. If I hadn't been such a "tough guy" on the outside—I would have broken down and just cried. Like a real man. Yes—real men cry. And real men are allowed to have emotions, but soldiers are not. I took deep breath after deep breath, trying to keep it together.

One of our guys interpreted what was going on differently.

"What the hell are these guys doing—taking their gear?"

I pretended not to hear it. I was a little confused, maybe even slightly disturbed, but I felt the stabbing pain coming from the SEALs as they cried and mourned over their brothers. Part of it was utilitarian; they needed supplies. Part of it was mourning and grief. Best for us not to judge what was right or wrong. My emotional gas tank was already on empty. I needed to just keep moving forward.

"Fuck this!" I heard from a fellow Ranger as he got up and walked into the wood line, presumably to get out of sight of the staged body bags. I couldn't blame him any more than I could blame the SEALs bent over in anguish or the ones grabbing a little extra gear. In times like these, we all just did what each of us needed to do. Let's face it—none of this stuff made the "regulations" handbook. Hell, none of us had faced mass death like this; most of us were in our early twenties and, frankly, hadn't experienced death, period. What context, what protocol, what preparation was there for anything as horrific as this?

My platoon leader, Lieutenant Howell, looked us in the eyes. Surely he'd picked up the strange vibes, but he knew our mission wasn't about grieving. It was about finding the missing four.

"This is a very hostile area, so be ready for a fight," he said. "SEAL Team 10 will take the lead. First and Third Squad with guns attached will join."

We had only a few hours of scorching daylight remaining to find these four men before darkness set in. About the time I was wondering what shape we'd find them in, Howell suggested he wasn't particularly hopeful.

"We expect them to be badly injured. Make sure we have our litter and medical supplies."

I handed some spare batteries for night vision to my team leader, Lucas.

"We're gonna be moving fast," said Masters. "Really fast. These guys can't last much longer out here. Not with this weather—with this terrain—with the carnage we've already seen. Make sure you guys are ready in five and be prepared to use severe noise discipline. We need to move fast but do it as quietly as possible. Let's go!"

He seemed oddly rushed. Like he knew something more than we did. For a guy who was almost always calm and collected, he seemed out of sorts. Was anyone else picking up this vibe other than me?

Lucas checked up on me as I was franticly checking my gear and litter. I was overloaded with ammo; that's exactly how I wanted it and how he wanted it.

I watched as SEAL Team 10 headed out of the open landing zone to our west. They were being counted out of our patrol base by none other than First Sergeant Garganta. That brick of pissed-off Army Ranger was a welcome sight. I watched as he counted each and every SEAL, then tapped each of us Rangers on the top of his helmet as we walked purposefully beyond the thick tree line.

We headed off, our silence steeled in the sanctity of loss. Thoughts of what might be awaited us ahead as we picked up the pace. Thoughts of victory, of failure. I couldn't help but think of the families. Of the kids that didn't have a father after today. Not only was I hoping to be a father someday, but I couldn't fathom having a tragedy take my father from me. I would have tried to rip the entire country of Afghanistan off of the map. The thoughts of never getting a chance to play catch with my future son or to scare the first boyfriend of my future daughter haunted me. We had little time to waste. But time, obviously, wasn't on our side.

My eyelids were heavy, my legs like Jell-O, my mouth parched, my uniform moist and covered in dirt. So what? I was a Ranger. Time to drive on.

I glanced back at the sixteen, accepting what I couldn't understand, and followed my orders, soon disappearing into the dark of the cedar forest.

HLZ Thresher looking up toward Sawtalo Sar. This is where we left the crash site to look for the four-man SEAL Recon element. (Courtesy of the Madslashers)

On HLZ Thresher. This is the area where we staged the crew of *Turbine 33* for their journey back home. (Courtesy of the Madslashers)

Hatfield and Hastings at HLZ Thresher. Hatfield showing off an Mk 48 while airing out his feet. (Courtesy of the Madslashers)

Peters and Hastings next to their shelter at HLZ Thresher. (Courtesy of Felipe Peters)

Second squad and our weapons squad. They secured the crash site and HLZ on first and third squad's departure for Chichal. (Courtesy of Felipe Peters)

12

THE LURE OF DANGER

SITREP: 48 hours since the crash of *Turbine 33*
East of Chichal, Afghanistan

WE HAD NOW BEEN ON SAWTALO SAR FOR SIXTEEN hours, hadn't slept in nearly two days, and were hoping against all odds that our search was going to find Luttrell, Murphy, Dietz, and Axelson alive. I'd seen enough dead US soldiers and sailors; I wanted to find guys with still-beating hearts.

We had only learned of the four-man reconnaissance team being on the run once we reached the crash site. We knew they'd called for help, but their whereabouts were unknown. I guess info was only being passed on to us on a need-to-know basis. And our primary mission hadn't initially involved that recon element. Now it did.

To the left, then right, I scanned the thick tree line for any sign of enemy movement. It was hard seeing further than about twenty-five meters into the thick trees. I would occasionally get a view of a goat trail up ahead, or the valley below. Mostly, I looked at Sal and the trail ahead of me.

Sal was moving at a brisk pace that had me jogging slightly at times. If I wasn't paying attention, he'd begin to pull away with his much longer legs. We'd walk a short distance on a trail, then slide a short distance on our rear ends, quickly descending toward the Korangal Valley below. I was hoping it wouldn't be the proverbial valley of death.

Minutes turned to dozens of minutes which quickly turned to hours of walking downhill. It was late afternoon and the slope of the mountain was steep. *Step. Step. Slide. Step. Step. Slide.* The rhythm was as disjointed as it was dangerous; the mountain, not I, seemed to be in control.

Halt! The back of Sal's hand brought us to a stop. He took a knee. I did the same—under a large pine. To our right flank I could only see straight down, to the Korangal Valley. We were on a goat trail that was swinging ninety degrees to our right. I noticed some rocks just ahead of me; they looked like a good spot for cover if I needed it.

As I rested, I noticed it: the scar on my finger. My mind quickly flashed back to when I'd been maybe ten and, like most boys I knew at the time, I wanted to make a spear. I wanted to be a warrior. So, while my father was away at work, I'd hacked off some branches from some giant shrubs he'd planted and nurtured. It was, as you might expect, one of those "seemed-like-a-good-idea-at-the-time" endeavors.

I needed something to take off the branches to make my spear, so I went to Mom.

"Can I get a knife so I can make a spear?" I said, as if I were asking for nothing more than crayons to draw a picture.

"Of course not, Anthony," she said. "That's dangerous."

To which I wanted to say: "Well, *duh*."

Isn't that why boys like to make spears? Because it's danger-ous? Wasn't that part of the reason I was on Sawtalo Sar at this very moment? Because it was dangerous? Wasn't that why, when Mom nixed the idea of loaning me a steak knife, I went into my father's den, rummaged around, and snuck a pair of scissors outside in an attempt to cut the twigs off the branch? And isn't that why I'd wound up nearly severing what someday would be my trigger finger? Why blood was flowing and I was lying on the grass, having nearly fainted, until my aunt pulled up for a visit, saw me, and rushed me inside?

At some level, I believe most males are built to fight. To go to battle. To try to make spears out of their father's prized bushes using only a pair of scissors.

Here's what will seem like a contradiction: *I hate war*. There is nothing to love about it. Some of my close friends may argue with me about that and claim to love it, but at the end of the day, we would still be drinking beers and giving bro hugs. Many of us loved the *idea* of war, the boyhood-imbued thoughts of glory and heroism. We loved the camaraderie, the brotherhood, the warrior spirit. Lacing up of combat boots, bearing armor, and fighting to the death. It was sexy. Hell, they made video games about war that made billions of dollars.

There's just one problem. Those games don't impart to the game-players the fear of being stuck on a mountain with no food or water, the smell of burning bodies, the despair in the wake of death.

As much as I thought I loved war while I trained up to fight an enemy, I had already—in just a few years—grown to hate it. What's more, I had watched some of my brothers in arms ship their sons off to fight in a war that they, themselves, had fought in almost two decades prior. And sadly, the war started before they were born. Think about it. Two generations, fighting the same enemy, in the same war, in the same country, the younger generation having been conceived after the war had begun. We have been in Afghanistan for two decades—and that's unacceptable. Warriors can only fight for so long before they are gassed. That's why all combat sports have a time limit before someone intervenes and says, "that is enough."

In 2011, Sergeant First Class Kristoffer Bryan Domeij, who was involved with Red Wings II, was killed in action by an IED while on his 14th combat deployment. He had spent nearly five years of his life in a combat zone and was known as one of the most deployed soldiers to be KIA in the Global War on Terror. How could anyone think that is a good idea? If you served in 2nd Ranger Battalion during the war on terror from 2001–2011, you knew Kris. He was the kind soul and ruthless JTAC that would wreak havoc on our enemies for over a decade. I am honored to have served with him and am filled with rage that he left us so soon.

It sickens me to think of two generations of a family losing people to the same war. Eighteen, nineteen, twenty years after the war began. While I sat on that mountain, I had no idea how long this war would last. I was only worried about the task at hand. Getting some damn sleep and getting home with my brothers.

But sometimes you have to do what you don't want to do—to protect the greater good. And, unfortunately, that often involved death.

THE LURE OF DANGER

NOW, ON SAWTALO SAR, THE AIR WAS HOT AND CRISP, the woods quiet. We had shed our body armor and were on the move. At any moment, I expected the crack of a rifle. My finger—the one I'd nearly severed as a kid—rested on the cold magazine well of my M4 Carbine. My eyes were fixed in the distance, scanning, sweeping back and forth. As I stared into a maze of pines, my heart rate increased, the sweat still pouring down my brow line, nose, and chin. Suddenly, I felt a slap on my left shoulder.

"Fuck!" I muttered under my breath as I nearly jumped out of my skin.

It was Lucas, my team leader. My drawers survived—this time.

"You just scared the shit out of me!"

"The first transponder hit was georeferenced right here. We're going to push out to our flanks a bit to see if anything is out here. And be cautious. The guys ahead are reporting bunkers all over the hills."

You didn't need to be Einstein to figure this one out. Either the transponder hit had been from one of our guys and he was still alive—or it was from the enemy who'd likely killed the man and was using the transponder hit to draw us in as prey.

Lucas pointed to the right flank, which featured a steep drop-off that made it feel as if you were looking down from atop a skyscraper. I brought my M4 to the "low ready" position. Slowly, but smoothly, I moved toward the steep decline. I needed to be sure there wasn't a way through which the enemy could approach. I crept beyond a rock pile, hid behind this tree then that one, and ultimately paused at the ledge. I looked back over my left shoulder.

Oh, my God. That was no rock pile. It was a machine-gun nest. My heart pounded. It wasn't just great cover; it was a fortified bunker so well disguised that I had knelt ten feet from it and not even noticed. Within a few feet was the rear of a man-made machine-gun bunker, dating back, I supposed, to the 1980s when soldiers in the Soviet-Afghan War were engaged in guerrilla warfare. Now, unfortunately, the bunkers were finding a second life.

War is a necessary evil—and, in some ways, more humane (if that's possible) than in centuries gone by, when Native American tribes would disembowel the enemy and tie them to trees by their intestines—or, for that matter, when, during the Spanish Inquisition, infidels were burned alive or sawed in half. But I didn't have to like anything about it. Or the fact that great men and women must give their lives as a result. As much as it feels like war represents unnecessary death, maybe those who die on the battlefield serve a bigger purpose. And for that reason, I have a healthy respect for it—even if I hate it.

It's much like I hate that firefighters die trying to pull humans from burning buildings. That's awful! However, I am grateful that someone is willing to jump into the fire to change the course of history for the people who might have otherwise died. Nobody likes the idea that firefighters sometimes die, but everybody appreciates that someone puts themselves on the line for others.

I scanned the small fortification. Could this have been what the Navy SEAL reconnaissance team of Murphy, Dietz, Axelson, and Luttrell had faced? God forbid that they faced a dug-in enemy on this terrain. Even the best of fighters would only have a snowball's chance in hell. As I looked around, I realized these bunkers were scattered, strategically, all over this godforsaken mountain. I was ten feet from a fighting position that could have rained hell upon everyone in my squad and the members of SEAL Team 10 just ahead of me.

A BUNCH OF RANGERS FINDING A SEAL TEAM HAD ALL sorts of implications. It's incredible how competitive every unit of the military was. We all were convinced ours was the best, the fittest, the smartest, the ballsiest. And that's exactly how it should be. In the gym, working out, in the bars, drinking hard, we'd always flip crap to each other; it was as if that was an expectation that we were required to fulfill. It was fun. But there were times—and this was one of them—when you realized we were all on the same team, fighting for the same thing. Bottom line: I just wanted the SEALs safe. And home. If we could be the unit to make that happen, all the better. It was no longer about pride, it was about leaving no man behind, regardless of what unit he was from and we were from.

We got word that one more georeferenced transponder hit was just below our current position. We moved further down the mountain, hoping that we would find what we were looking for—the four-man Navy SEAL reconnaissance team. We followed the goat trails etched into the mountainside in switchbacks. All of it was covered in thick pines, sprinkled with bunkers that didn't look like bunkers because they'd been so cagily crafted. Each reminded me where I was: in a war zone. A war zone that knew fighting for longer than I'd been around. Every time I passed one, my mortality bled into my conscious thought.

We traversed down to a small, flat area from which we suspected the second transponder hit was coming. We hurriedly set up an oblong-shaped security halt and, on a single knee, started scanning the terrain for any signs of life, or a fight, anything that spoke of The Four.

When Staff Sergeant Masters reported that "there's nothin' here," you could feel whatever energy was left in our men wither completely. As if tripped by a switch, you could hear the rancor rise. Verbal sparring. Guys taking out their frustration on each other. Where else were they supposed to vent their anger, except on each other? Emotions were on edge. Frustration was setting in. Even our leaders were squabbling with each other. When Sgt.First Class Congdon entered the dispute, things started to calm down. No surprise to me. No one wanted to confront Congdon—that is, if they had anything occupying the space between their two ears.

I melted into the ground. I polished off the last of my water, my legs all Gumby-like, my back like a pack mule's. It had been more than two full days since the SEALs' initial call for help. We would later learn that multiple calls had been attempted by the team, from both radio and satellite phone. Likely coming from Danny Dietz, the SEAL team's radio operator, and Michael Murphy, the team leader. While I can't definitively say who made the calls, it would seem likely both were letting it be known they'd run into enemy resistance. This, I would later learn, was likely why we'd had multiple locations to search—the places from which evidence showed they'd attempted radio transmissions or satellite phone calls. We know that radio checks were made along the SEAL team's route, and that Michael Murphy made a satellite call as noted in his Medal of Honor citation.

But now the search was clearly over—at least for our platoon at the moment.

"We're headed back up," said Sgt. Jones. "We need to hurry the fuck up because they want to turn this mountain into a glass parking lot." In other words, leadership was planning on bombing in the area. A lot of bombs that would heat the sand on the ground. I was bummed. I think all of us were. We were leaving empty handed. No SEALs to bring home—alive.

As we headed back up the mountain to the site of the crash and the helicopter landing zone, we were all struggling. I was on empty. Simply putting one foot in front of the other was hard. I was out of water and my mouth and lips were dry and parched. Half a mile below our destination, I went to a knee, clearly at my breaking point.

Sal walked up to me. "Give me the sked," he said.

It was shameful to not pull your weight as a Ranger. I certainly didn't want to show any weakness. None of us ever did. I resisted, my body language suggesting I wasn't about to give up the stretcher I was carrying.

"Give it to me, dammit," he said. "Now."

OK, I was convinced. He really wanted it. I got that damn backpack Skedco off my back in record time. Sal didn't skip a beat. He threw it on his back, then helped me to my feet.

I was reinvigorated and ready to get back. I looked up ahead and saw two men still on a knee—the machine-gun team for the SEAL team. To be fair, that gun was not light. Still. Sager and Torres walked past the two as if hardly breathing. As I passed them, I heard the assistant gunner trying to fire up his gunner buddy. "C'mon man, you got this. Let's fucking go!"

Congdon, the guy so big he offered me much-needed shade, was walking back down to make sure our guys weren't lagging.

"Doesn't it make you feel good?" he asked. I wasn't sure if he was referring to being close to our destination or seeing that we weren't stalled like the SEAL machine-gun team. Either way, yeah, it did.

We made it back just as the sun was setting. First Sgt. Garganta was there to count us into the patrol base, slapping us hard on our helmets. In a war zone, it was the closest thing we were going to get to a hug. I don't want to go all Kumbaya on you or anything, but, damn, it felt good.

Now we waited. And waited. And waited. We were told that the 160th MH-47 would be landing any minute. Those minutes became hours. The bird finally arrived near midnight. Pitch black. Even with my PVS-14, I could only see the helicopter coming in for a quick touch down.

Physically, we were cutting it. Mentally, we were frayed like century-old rope. Our leaders had been squawking with SEAL Team 10, which had their undies in a bunch about not being able to find their four brethren. At the time, I might not have cut them much slack, but now I get it: *the four out there were their guys.* Our cousins, but their *brothers.* Guys who'd trained and worked and drank together, sealed by blood, sweat, and tears.

This time, SEAL Team 10 insisted on taking its own guys out with them—the guys who'd died in the helicopter. They were to load their fallen brothers onto the very same type of aircraft that they'd been on when shot out of the sky. The SEALs worked fast. They had all sixteen body bags and their entire team on that bird in less than two minutes. As the bird lifted away, I held my breath. Thankfully, they were out of Dodge in seconds—no enemy fire to add to what was already looking like two nightmares: four MIA SEALs and sixteen of their would-be rescuers dead. I exhaled and finally felt a sliver of contentedness. Contentedness that the Sixteen were headed home where they belonged. To their loved ones.

Then my emotions spiraled into a twisting of virtually every feeling you could have: Disappointment. Anger. Confusion. Sadness. Guilt. We'd accomplished nothing, really. SEAL Team 10 had taken its dead; it had been our job to try to find the four who still might be alive: Luttrell, Murphy, Dietz, and Axelson. But, by now, that was looking fairly hopeless.

In the Hollywood version of war, the good guys inevitably lose people. But, in the end, it's always, "Mission Accomplished." Not so in real-life war, in real-death war. Sometimes all your training, all your planning, all your energy and strategy and effort produces something that bothers me to even write: *failure.*

I hate failure. I hate to lose. Always have. Always will.

That's why I became a Ranger. Well, that and because, like using scissors to make a homemade spear, it was dangerous.

On the side of a mountain, I lay down and tried to get some shut-eye, having morphed into two versions of myself: the little boy with his homemade spear and the young man who'd already seen too much.

13

THE STARS ALIGNED

SITREP: 53 hours since the crash of *Turbine 33*
HLZ Thresher, just west of the crash site, Afghanistan

IT WOULD BE MY LONGEST NIGHT EVER. WE WERE ON the side of a mountain, in a place draped in desolation. We had not slept in more than two days. I stared up at the stars, thinking about what I would be doing if I was back in the States. I imagined myself over a candlelit dinner with The Unicorn, but that flicker of hope now seemed way farther away than the nearly 7,000 miles it actually was.

June 30, 2005, was coming to an inglorious ending, my mind fogged by a physical and mental twisting of fortune and fate not going our way. We knew we were in the enemy's back yard. And we felt the frustration of having not engaged that enemy once; hell, hadn't even *seen* the enemy, minus a short blast from an A-10 "Hawg."

I was flat-out pissed. And for some reason, a lot of my anger, I later realized, was rooted back in America, where too many people didn't give a rat's ass for a mission that, to me, was the most honorable thing I'd ever done: putting my life on the line for my country.

Now, I've never seen what I did as heroic, nor was my motive in joining the Rangers ever about glory. But, hell yes, I wanted someone to care that I was here. That my buddies were here. That those sixteen men who'd just been flown off in body bags had just been here. And that the four men who we were still searching for were out there somewhere in the Afghan wilderness, dead or alive.

That said, as I lay there, chiseled into the side of that Afghan mountain, I couldn't help but think of this huge chasm between me and much of the country I was serving.

It angered me to think of coming home to people who might not care less if I walked off that big bird at Fort Lewis or if I came home in a casket. My death would be a blip on their radar—or just a reason to change the channel. Like all people, I wanted to *matter*. But when you're in the military, you experience the strangest dichotomy. You find yourself mattering a lot to the men around you—and having them matter to you in the same way. Every day, even in training, your lives depend on each other.

At the same time this bond was strengthening within our unit, however, our bond with civilians was weakening. Part of that is natural, of course. You were with the other guys in the unit 24/7 and you were with civilians only when you grabbed a beer on your rare days off during training back home. And once we headed to Afghanistan, of course, even that limited opportunity to interact with civilians was gone.

Since joining the military, I'd come to believe that a lot of civilians wanted the benefits of freedom but weren't the least bit concerned about the cost. Whenever the topic of budgets comes up, the first thing I hear is something about the cost of war and the Department of Defense budget. This isn't a liberal-vs.-conservative debate as much as an understanding of why Americans enjoy the freedom they do: *because we invest deeply in protecting that freedom with military personnel, training, and equipment. Strength is a natural deterrent to conflict.*

When America was attacked at Pearl Harbor, our collective resistance—refusal to look the other way—wrapped civilians and soldiers in a common purpose: *to protect the good of the nation.* Did the country sometimes go too far in its response to the attack? Unfortunately, yes; the rounding up of Japanese Americans and forcing them into internment camps was a step too far. We got caught up in the emotion of fear. But, for the most part, the war stitched civilians and soldiers together in a way America hasn't seen since.

Vietnam was tremendously divisive—and for good reason: Soldiers and citizens alike were being lied to by US leaders who were having us fight a war to save face at the cost of nearly 60,000 US lives. The Global War on Terrorism in Iraq and Afghanistan hasn't been particularly divisive; instead, what's driven the wedge between civilian and soldier has been non-chalance, ignorance, a collective shrug of the shoulders from civilians. After the terrorist attacks on America on September 11, 2001, civilians forgot in a hurry where this hatred toward us was rooted. Innocent people—nearly 3,000 people from ninety different countries—were peacefully going about their everyday lives when they were viciously murdered by nineteen aggressors.

Since soon after that attack, American soldiers have been deploying for Afghanistan, then Iraq. But how soon we forget. Because, unlike Vietnam, the soldiers who went to Iraq and

Afghanistan were all volunteers, and so the war on terror has been much easier to ignore.

When civilians and soldiers are on the same page, it's easier for everyone. There's trust. There's respect. There's understanding. But we've lost that. Now, there's no sense of villagers sending off their warriors to protect the interests of freedom for all, then welcoming back with open arms, and deep thanks, those who survive the battle. There's no collective grieving for the ones who didn't make it home, just the Memorial Day guilt of barbecuing instead of bowing your head in a cemetery. Instead, soldiers have gradually become this oddity in America; in 2015, less than one percent of all Americans were serving in the military. Less than one percent!

We have become ghosts. We come and go. We do what we can to preserve what I think most people value highly: their freedom. But at times we feel like someone's air-conditioning system: something people notice only if something goes wrong and it inconveniences them personally.

Like when a helicopter with sixteen men goes down. I knew that would make headlines. But the day-to-day sacrifices military personnel make—nope. And I knew it would be the same way we'd come home: nobody would notice unless something went wrong. It would be as if we'd never left. Then some guy wracked with PTSD because of his time in Iraq and/or Afghanistan would go on a shooting spree and, bingo: headlines.

"GET SOME REST," MASTERS TOLD US. "COULD BE A long night."

SEAL Team 10 had just extracted its brethren and was headed to a nearby forward operating base (FOB). If we needed help, if 2nd Platoon from Charlie Company 2/75 weren't enough backup, a call to "10" would provide an additional quick reaction force.

As much disappointment as I felt when they left the mountain, I did not give up hope. I'm a born optimist. A little bit of hope goes a long way. A little bit of hope with the correct person can change humanity. At least in this case, a little bit of hope could result in someone coming home. Alive.

Even just one.

I was facing to the east, with the site of *Turbine 33*'s crash directly on my left at my 9 o'clock and my attached Mk-48 machine gun team at my 10 o'clock. Nothing but me, my uniform, and my rifle. No sleeping bag or campfire. However, the smell of the recent fires from the crash of *Turbine 33* still permeated the air. I found cover between an outcropping of rocks.

A slight throbbing pulsed from my feet, a precursor to blisters and a reminder of the ground that those two feet had slapped for the past twenty-four hours. This is what we trained for—the type of mission that only a few select units could handle. Many of them could not get two platoons up in this terrain as fast as we did, if at all. I couldn't say enough about guys to my right and left.

I was on first watch. Lucas reminded me of that in no uncertain terms. He looked me in the eyes and said, "You're the only person who's gonna be awake. If we get killed, I will *kill* you."

Point well taken. I believed him. I genuinely thought that if something happened on my watch, he would rise from the dead and take me out because of my stupid mistake. It was a healthy fear. I had more fear of failing him than I feared anything else. I respected him greatly and knew his character to be that of an outstanding leader, mentor, and a genuinely great person.

As I lay prone under the dark, star-lit canopy, I let my eyes wander to distract myself from the events of the day. The temperature had come down considerably, but it was still comfortable, probably in the mid- to low-70s. After a warm day of temperatures near the century mark, it was a welcome break. I just lay there, pulling security above the vast valley below while processing all that had happened in a short slice of time.

I could still see the faces of all the men who we had recovered just hours before; it was as if they were physically burned into my retinas. I thought of their families. My brain could not let go of all of the people that this event had already touched—all who would be touched. The thought stung like the hundreds of hornets that had attacked me a few months prior in training. I'd take those physical stings over this situation a thousand times over.

I could see for miles and miles over the valley below as if I was standing on the roof of the tallest building in town, but, at this elevation, a building that was 500 stories high. The terrain seemed to go on forever like an ocean of dirt and sand.

I could see small village huts below, maybe ten of them, but I couldn't see any movement. It was as if the entire village was vacant. I looked for any sign of life. Any sign of danger. They were far away, probably 5,000 feet linearly from my location and nearly 5,000-plus feet below me. I couldn't be effective at that distance—not with my weaponry—even if I was the best of shooters.

In reality, my search for the enemy was reminiscent of how we ended the day: empty handed. Regardless, I diligently made some mental notes on distances and directions of as many avenues of approach that the enemy could possibly take to make our day worse. If anyone decided to walk up this particular side of the mountain, there was absolutely no cover for the first thousand feet directly in front of me. It was like a target range back home at Fort Lewis. If I needed to take a shot, nothing would be in my way.

While I was looking through the green hue of my night-vision monocular, something caught my attention: what appeared to be some sort of infrared laser to my 9 o'clock. It was pointed directly up at the sky and was circling as if it were trying to lasso something. *Wait—is that one of the four SEALs?*

"Lucas, can you see that laser?" I asked our team leader. "Is it one of our guys?"

He quickly agreed it could be and passed up the information about what we were seeing. In that moment, I felt a sense of excitement and pride that someone may have survived this mess. *Maybe it is one of the SEALs,* I thought to myself. It was far away—we would take a full day to get there. I mentally prepared myself for what I believed would have to be a follow-on patrol. *We had to check this out,* I thought. The air assets above could look into it, but they could only see so much through the tree-covered terrain. It would be up to us to make the confirmation.

"They see it," said Lucas. "No one has any word about where it's coming from yet."

It seemed to be coming from the direction of the Shuryek Valley to our north. It had already been a few days since the initial call for assistance from the four main SEAL recon team, so time was not on our side, nor on the foursome's.

Out of nowhere, my stomach let out a gremlin-esque growl. Nothing too concerning, but it had been over twenty-four hours since my last meal. I had eaten a high quality, five-star military meal, a chili mac MRE (Meal, Ready-to-Eat) back in Jalalabad. Food wasn't really atop my priority list and I was notorious for going on long fasts, so hunger wasn't a problem for me.

We had been replenished with some water by the 160th crew during the extraction of the sixteen passengers and crew of *Turbine 33* a few hours prior. I was drinking as much as I could stomach during this period of rest. But I was more concerned about the condition of my legs and feet. I had heard rumblings from a few guys whose feet were toast. Hatfield had been walking gingerly earlier, but I didn't think anything of it at the time.

There was talk that we were in the area where the SEAL recon team had been. I glanced over to my left to see "Big Todd," who carried our team's Mk 46 machine gun. Most infantry units just call it the squad automatic weapon or SAW (pronounced like the cutting tool). It was always nice to know that Todd was nearby. He could handle that SAW in about any situation and put down a hail of gunfire with a few short squeezes of his pointer finger. He was one of my "security blankets."

As infantrymen, we always defaulted toward firepower. It was one of the things that helped us sleep at night. Firepower to us was like a teddy bear to a small child. Comforting. Safe. Todd was trying to sleep at the moment, so I was sitting behind his SAW, just scanning—to my left and to my right, trying to be the first Ranger to see an insurgent attempting to walk into our Vietnam-style patrol base. We all would relish being able to take the first shot at the men responsible for this carnage. Assuming, of course, that the Air Force hadn't already take care of that for us earlier in the day.

After two and a half hours behind the Mk 46 squad automatic weapon, I watched the laser lassoing the sky in the distance. Lucas walked over and sat next to me.

"Hey—it sounds like we're going to go on offense tomorrow. They're talking about patrols and potential ordnance drops in the area. Make sure you're hydrating and taking care of your feet. We need to find those SEALs."

"Can these guys still be alive?" I asked. "It is pretty fucked up that we still don't know where they are. Better find 'em soon."

Lucas ignored me. He stared straight into my face and pointed to the ground behind the line. His silence said exactly what I didn't want to hear. The unknown. The fear of failure still loomed.

"Get some rest," he said.

I passed on my duties behind the machine gun to the next guy in my squad and moved behind the line of our patrol base. My M4 Carbine sat to my side and I was lying flat on the ground, staring up at the insanely bright stars above. In the eerie dead of the night, the only sound was that of a slight breeze through the trees.

Suddenly: a scream. The loudest, most high-pitched and hair-raising shrill of a scream that's ever slapped me in the face. Every single hair on my body stood on edge and an instant adrenaline rush hit as if I'd just seen a ghost. I bolted to the ready like a neighborhood dog who had just spotted an intruder. Ready to pounce. My first thought: a fighter had breached our patrol base and attacked one of our guys. I popped up, grabbed my M4 and looked at my team leader for guidance. The radio chattered to life.

"What the fuck was that?" I asked Lucas.

He put his palm up in my face as if to tell me to shut up. The radio squawked again. I heard the voice of our Platoon Sergeant, Congdon.

"Tell that guy to be quiet over there," I heard Congdon say over the radio.

I didn't have a radio that picked up the platoon frequency, so I could only hear a bit from the headset that lay next to me on the ground. The rest was unintelligible. If you've ever been on a military radio, you understand that some voices are easy to understand while others sound as if coming from someone talking while eating a banana and using a chainsaw.

Word came down—the scream had been that of one of our guys who'd encountered a monkey or a bobcat apparently sprinting past a section of the patrol base that was occupied by our third squad.

I didn't catch more than a few minutes of shut eye. Beyond the *Friday the 13th* scream, I couldn't shake the images of the *Turbine 33* crew. Combine that with a little dehydration and thoughts of enemy fighters ready to pounce and I ended up mostly looking up at the stars and that laser off in the distance. I couldn't help but wonder if that was our crew of SEALs evading the enemy's grip.

While I lay in wait of a little shut eye, little did I know that back home The Unicorn was doing the same thing when night arrived in the Pacific Northwest. But unlike me, she didn't have a worry on her mind.

14

REVENGE OF THE JDAMS

SITREP: 63 hours since the crash of *Turbine 33*
HLZ Thresher

THE BITING COLD OF DAWN CAME SWIFTLY, THE CHAT-
tering of my teeth offering a morning drumbeat. Better, I suppose, than the silence of the night—punctuated by that scream we'd heard. I had slept—really slept—for an estimated eleven minutes.

We were all on edge. Two nights, almost three without sleep can do that to the strongest of humans. The radio began to squawk, most of it unintelligible, but not all. Imposters were having a field day.

"Can you believe this shit?" said one of the radio operators near command headquarters. "It was the thickest Pashtun accent I've ever heard claiming that they were 'The American.'"

I chuckled. It reminded me of stories I'd heard about the Vietcong sending fake radio transmissions to lure US troops into danger. Isn't it ironic? We had Vietnam-style radio transmissions in Afghanistan—in our Vietnam-style patrol base. We were thick in the middle of another seemingly unwinnable war that dragged on like some endless winter, a war that wasn't about liberating villages or gaining ground as in World War II. Not about definable stuff. More like a sophisticated game of Whack-a-Mole. The rodent pops up here; *boom.* The rodent pops up there; *boom.*

Had we made some progress? Of course. Our military was head and shoulders above our enemy. We had the technology, weaponry, and a significant physical advantage. We had every asset known to man available to us. But the enemy had something we didn't: familiarity with the terrain. And knowledge of the weather and the heat that would further dehydrate us on this day.

They lived here. Every tree was familiar, every crag and crevice of the mountain memorized in their minds. They could slowly and systematically wreak havoc on our troops. Pick us off, one man at a time. They had unlimited patience; for them, war was a way of life, 24/7, year after year, decade after decade. They had made fighting a "lifestyle choice."

We were here on a temporary basis. Just like in the old days when the Soviets would send their government-trained, professional athletes to compete in the Olympics against US athletes who quit their summer jobs at the burger shack long enough to go beat the world's best. At least that's what we believed. We were on a diet of sorts. Hoping to get back to our normal high-carb, high-fat, full-of-crap "Standard American Diet" in a few months. *And boy, wouldn't an In-N-Out burger be nice right about now?*

What's more, the two of us played by different rules. We didn't have the political permission to win this war. We were handcuffed with "rules of engagement," always worried about being prosecuted for our actions in war—if not in military court then in the media. The enemy? Hell, they played by their own rules, worried not a twit about the media, and made their own justice.

The enemy was living lawlessly. They were fighting to survive; we were fighting to preserve freedom—but fighting while restricted. Politics. Media. Responsibility. I know this will sound weird, but *consciences*. None of it was inherently bad, but in war all worked against us. I could see the headline now: MH-47 CARRYING 16 SHOT DOWN IN AFGHANISTAN. FOUR NAVY SEALs MISSING IN ACTION. Later, I'd find that was exactly what the headlines said. I could never get a grip on why this would be reported to civilians. Why tell them at all? It isn't news to a civilian. It only drives anxiety, and discord for the tasks at hand. After all, did they report the eight to ten terrorists who we wiped off the map a day later? Nope. Not one word.

IT WAS GROWING CLEAR TO US THAT THE ENEMY HAD done the smart thing when we arrived: gotten out of town. It was a tactic with which Rangers were familiar. The indigenous population knew us by our uniforms and equipment, by the type of night-bird insertions we used to get onto this mountain. The enemy was smart. Their motto was: "Don't mess with the guys who come at night."

I remember telling my father that, when I deployed, I was going to be one of the safest people in the country. I meant that. The enemy identified Special Operations fairly well. When they saw us in their area, they generally chose to hide and live to fight another day. They chose to pick their fights with conventional units with fewer assets and inferior weaponry and training. They chose to fight "safe."

"Dad, the enemy knows who we are. They don't want to fight Mike Tyson. They would rather fight the next guy who comes their way."

Back on the mountain, I overheard more scuttlebutt from platoon headquarters.

"They're gonna drop some munitions on a local village. Sounds like we need to hold tight until they drop and then chase."

Here we go, I thought. If they were dropping 500-pound bombs, they must have some great intel on the scumbags who had downed the helicopter. *Wait. What about the SEALs? Couldn't they be in harm's way?*

"Hey, Sarn't Lucas," I said. "Do we know where our guys are? Seems odd that they would drop bombs when we still don't know where the SEALs are located—am I right?"

My face was mildly contorted into confusion, eyes squinting.

"Don't know. We'll be heading out soon to check out a few locations. They may have us search the bomb site also. I think they know where these guys came from."

Lucas pointed to our north and east—toward the remnants of *Turbine 33*, tail number 146. That was enough for me. I was uneasy but trusted that someone in higher command had more information than we did—than *I* did—about our missing SEAL team. At least they seemed to know where our boys were *not*. They were not where these bombs were headed—apparently.

Nearby, Hatfield was airing out his feet. "Hey, Hatty. What-cha think about the bombs? Any chance they know where this asshole is who did this?"

That's when I saw it: his bare foot, the bottom of which looked like he'd taken a cheese grater to it.

"Holy shit, dude! What the hell happened to your foot? Have you seen Doc?"

"Not yet. Trying to air it out a bit before we have to move out. It's fine. Don't worry about it. And to answer your question: they're gonna rain hell upon this asshole."

We both just smiled and stared at his raw hamburger of a foot. That was the moment when I realized how lucky I was to have chosen my Danner boots instead of my Oakley assault boots for this mission. If Hatfield had known how brutal our walk into the crash site was going to be, he would never have chosen the soft and flexible Oakley. Then again, hindsight was always 20/20. Now Hatfield was paying a painful price for prioritizing comfort instead of durability.

And, oh, the smell of our feet: Whenever someone popped their boots off, it smelled like a dying Sasquatch after eating East Indian cuisine.

SITREP: 72 hours since the crash of *Turbine 33*
HLZ Thresher

"HERE WE GO," SAID MASTERS AS HE PREPPED HIS gear. "Ten minutes till bombs on target. We are headed to the bomb site as soon as it hits. We need to verify that we got this asshole. And take care of anyone else in the area."

Now we're talking! We were geared up in minutes. Hatfield was still sitting with his feet out of his boots. Masters looked us all in the eyes and said each of our names: "Jones, Russell, Lucas, Salyer, Todd, Brooks, Torres, and Sager will be coming with me, company command, third squad, some RRD, Lt. Howell, and Congdon. We are headed to that bomb site once it hits."

Hatfield was not happy. He looked up in disappointment.

"Not going," he said. "My feet. They're done."

I hurt for the guy, but I totally got it: looking at his feet made me wince. He waddled over to a spot with more sun, hoping to dry out his feet as the temperature climbed.

Suddenly, I heard the sound of freedom swoosh overhead in the form of an F-16. Less than one minute later—*Boom! Boom! Boom!* You could feel the concussion of the bombs through your boots, as if the floor of Sawtalo Sar was a large bass drum and Zeus himself was on the sticks.

"Wow! Holy shit!" I instinctively responded as the impact rattled us all. The mood instantly shifted.

"Let's go!" Masters barked as we headed out northwest, toward the village of Chichal. High command believed Chichal was where Ahmad Shah, the anti-coalition leader, was based. Where he was building his IEDs to further terrorize our troops. Now we were tasked with finding evidence of his demise, and evidence of his men meeting their creator. All of us wanted him dead. You could tell by the extra bounce in our once-weary steps.

Then, info that only further pumped us up.

"Three Charlie has new intel," said Masters. "A local is claiming that they have a SEAL—alive."

15

UNDER
THE WATERFALL

I COULDN'T BELIEVE IT. ALL THE HOPE THAT HAD BEEN crushed up until this point didn't matter. One of our guys was apparently alive—at least that's what someone wanted us to believe. Was it a setup? We discussed the possibility but welcomed the opportunity to bring the fight. In fact, something felt natural about being the aggressor. Being the one that started and finished the fight. On our terms.

Maybe it was just me. This was my chance to control the situation. Unlike when my grandfather passed away when I was thirteen. I wasn't ready for that one. Hell, I wasn't ready for what I witnessed on this mountain a day ago.

But to imagine a dead enemy did not make me flinch. It was what I needed to close the door on my sorrow. I would later find it odd that I thought death would somehow bring closure to, well, *death*. Anger, I was beginning to realize, had a weird way of changing a person. That is why I was here. To avenge the deaths of innocent Americans on 9/11. In a weird way, the occupants of *Turbine 33* felt like innocent Americans. They were killed as they attempted to help their buddies out of a jam.

"Are we going to get him?" I asked Sergeant Jones, already giddy with the hope that the answer was yes.

"Three Charlie is going to investigate while we check out the JDAM site. It's too far for us to assist." A joint direct attack munition, or JDAM, was simply a guidance system that allowed bombs to have precision on target guidance. In other words, they hit their targets. This wasn't carpet bombing like we saw in 1939 in World War II when the German Luftwaffe laid waste to Warsaw, Poland, destroying nearly 85% of the city. This was a bomb that landed on an individual house, to target a specific *individual.*

Damn. We were already too far in the opposite direction to assist. As disappointed as I was, I knew the importance of the JDAM site and making sure that this crew of miscreants could no longer take the lives of Americans.

THE SUN WAS SETTING QUICKLY, COOLING US DOWN AS we sledged our way down the steep terrain, zig-zagging on switchbacks. At times, we slid on our butts because of the unforgiving terrain. I welcomed the dip in temperature from 100 degrees to a relatively cool 70. Rain began to trickle on us as we continued our descent. There it was: a halt sign from the man in front of me. We were stopping to transition into night vision. Just a brief stop to give our eyes a chance to adjust. Before I knew it, we were up and moving again.

Only now, the rain was picking up. From a mist to a steady pelting of Northwest-style, frog-choking, overflowing-gutter rain, the kind I remembered from Fort Lewis. It was already getting my gear wet, increasing the weight of everything. My once-light uniform was now like a suit of armor.

A shiver ran up my spine, part of it my suddenly being cold, part of it my fear of what that cold could mean to us while on an exposed mountainside. I'd read enough failed-rescue stories back home to know how quickly weather could put people in danger, particularly at high elevation. Never mind that I'd been sweating only an hour ago; the colder it got, the more concerned I got.

Soon the rain was coming down so hard I couldn't see the man in front of me. At times, it transitioned into all-out hail. At this point, we had already closed ranks to about ten-to-fifteen feet between us because of the darkness and the thick wood line. Now we needed to close the gap even further. I looked ahead and saw only sheets of water. In a slight panic, I picked up my pace in the direction I believed that the group was heading.

Shit. Where the fuck did they go?

Now my heart was racing. The rain had effectively separated me from the patrol, and I was in no man's land. I couldn't see the guy in front of me or behind me. I was nearly jogging when—*smack!*—I walked right into Big Todd. *Thank God!*

For the slightest moment, I thought I might have wandered away from the element. I placed my hand on Todd's backpack as we sloshed forward. The man behind me grabbed the top of the litter that was on my back, a small pond having formed in a crease.

Suddenly, the train ground to a halt.

"Why are we stopping?" someone asked from the rear.

I don't think anyone knew except for the men up front. It turned out, our company commander Pat Work, platoon leader Jimmy Howell, and platoon sergeant Congdon had surmised what I had, too: that this weather had the potential to send guys into hypothermia. We were completely combat ineffective. Captain Work was concerned for his men. He was a former Army middle linebacker who weighed probably sixty pounds more than I did. If he was cold—everyone was. We needed to hunker down and find a way to get warm.

We moved to nearby trees and were told to pull security. The forest floor was like a shallow lake. A fire was out of the question; we might as well send up a flare that exploded into a sky-written message with a giant arrow pointing at us: "Americans here." The rain pelted, the earth turned to sea, our uniforms became self-insulating freezers around our bodies.

It was like nothing I'd ever experienced. It was a combination of the coldness of the Northwest rain, but the hardness of the Arizona monsoons. An hour before, I was worried about sweating and overheating. Now my body had locked up as if my joints were packed in ice. As I lay on the ground, every muscle in my body twitched. I broke into a full-on, incessant "shiver fit."

My thoughts began fading into nothingness. My brain started to short out like a bad electrical wire. I got so cold I pulled my M4 under my chest and lay directly on it in an attempt to insulate my body from the ground. It wasn't logical. I knew it was metal and not an insulator. But my mind was beyond rational.

My only saving grace was the litter on my back. That damn thing was at least keeping a lot of the rain from directly pelting me. Todd was to my right, Sal to my left, and Lucas to his left. Five minutes became ten, ten became twenty. In all of my time in the military, including winter Ranger School, this was the first time I'd entertained the serious thought that I was going to die. This was the only moment when I felt genuinely scared. I honestly believed that I might freeze to death.

That's another misnomer that civilians have about the military: that the only way we put ourselves in harm's way is when we allow some enemy soldier to have us in the crosshairs of a rifle—or if we risk getting blown into a million pieces by an IED. In fact, more than seven in ten military deaths among those serving in Afghanistan and Iraq were "unrelated to war," according to a 2019 Congressional Research Service report.

Combat is just a small slice of a huge operation. Accidents happen in training. Vehicles crash. Guys get sick. Some take their own lives. The risk of being killed or injured while in the military goes well beyond the battlefield. And this moment was a reminder of exactly that; I honestly thought if this rain continued, some of us would die of hypothermia on this mountain.

With Iraq and Afghanistan, the linear combat theater flew out the window. Some combat troops rarely left a Forward Operating Base (FOB) and some non-combat personnel got shot at regularly. The Congressional Research Service reports that forty-five percent of all deaths in Afghanistan and Iraq from 2006–2019 were from IEDs.

The enemy put bombs on roads, on walls, in trees; hell, any place that they could hide a bomb, the enemy would. The impact of IEDs caused traumatic brain injury (TBI), an epidemic amongst our war fighters. According to the Veterans Administration, 22 percent of all combat casualties from these conflicts were brain injuries, compared to 12 percent of Vietnam-related combat casualties.

LEAVE NO MAN BEHIND

NOW, ON THE SIDE OF THAT MOUNTAIN, WE WERE HOPING to not become war casualties of weather. Weird as it might sound, I had the thought that my service member life insurance policy might actually pay out the $250,000 to my family. (In World War II, most soldiers' policies were for $10,000.) When you are in a war zone and your only thoughts are about finding a way to warm up, you know it's bad. I didn't have a single thought about fighting or, for that matter, being killed by an ambush. I could only think about getting warm again—and was worried what might happen if I didn't.

"Get out your space blankets or ponchos if you have them!" yelled Lucas over the din of the downpour. "Don't worry about security in this shit. No one is fighting out here. No one."

I had already turned that page in my book. I was struggling to get my body to cooperate with me. I knew that I had an emergency space blanket in my litter bag. However, my body would not react to my brain's commands to fetch it. *Just push up, take off the litter bag. Then get that space blanket out of the small front pocket, spread it over the top of you, and lay back down under it.* I just kept repeating the steps in my head. Again. And again. And again. My body wasn't having it.

"Todd, on my back," I said. "Grab that fucking space blanket."

Thankfully, Big Todd was much more capable than I was. The crinkling sound of the silver reflective blanket combined with the rain pelting it like a snare drum only solidified that we didn't give a shit about anything other than getting warm. Todd handed me a side of the blanket and we cuddled under that thing like two toddlers with a teddy bear. Only, Todd was my teddy bear.

Bet you've never read anything like that in a book about war, but that's the thing—too many books about war conform to stereotypes about soldiers that sometimes aren't true. Here's the truth: We get scared. We worry about dying. And, in life-or-death situations, we, well, *snuggle*. I hate to break this to you, but Rambo was a fictional character. Rambo was Sylvester Stallone, a guy who shot a scene, then was pampered in an air-conditioned trailer while he awaited another scene. He never took a bullet, never shivered on the side of a mountain, never worried about losing the chance to ask out the girl of his dreams.

Sal and Lucas brought over another space blanket and we all—with no care in the world other than getting warm—kept each other warm. It was a dog pile of big, strong warriors, helping each other stay alive with one another's body warmth. As the smallest guy in the bunch, I wiggled to the center of this get-warm party.

As the rain pounded and the night deepened, it got so cold that Captain Work decided the risk of giving away our presence was lower than the risk of our dying. We started a fire. Very risky, but in my opinion, a bold leadership move that kept us all alive. It was up and blazing in no time.

"Go dry off at the fire," Lucas ordered. "And hurry up."

As much as I not only wanted to be next to that fire but *in* that fire, I couldn't will myself to get up. I was having trouble getting to my feet. Others weren't waiting for my cognitive sensors to kick in. Todd and Lucas each grabbed an arm and helped me up. I stumbled over to the flames. I looked at the hot embers—and let them warm my body.

It felt like victory. I could feel every part of my body coming back to life, as if I was getting some sort of special serum. Steam rose from my uniform. I dried out surprisingly fast. But only because that fire was putting out some serious heat. So much heat that the ties at the bottom of my DCU pants melted.

I'm convinced two things saved me from death that night: first, being so desperate that we built a fire to keep warm and, second, the Ranger Indoctrination Program back in Georgia, where, above all, you learned to *will* yourself to stay alive to fight another day.

As I took a knee away from the fire, I had a new sense of purpose, quickly forgetting how miserable I'd been. I was going on three days without sleep. I was tired, but not as tired as I might have imagined. The renewed warmth of my body rejuvenated my spirits. We would be on the move shortly, traversing the most treacherous portion of the downhill climb into Chichal.

Meanwhile, I would not be among the seven in ten military people in Iraq or Afghanistan who died outside of combat.

16

A HAND IN THE RUBBLE

SITREP: 85 hours since the crash of *Turbine 33*
Chichal, Afghanistan

THE MORNING OF JULY 1, WE WERE STILL ON THE MOUN-
tain. Earlier, some of us thought if things went smoothly we
might be back in the States, able to blow off some steam at our
local watering hole this Friday night. But things had not gone
smoothly. So, there would be no homecoming with our loved
ones, family, and friends. No chance to hit up The Unicorn for
that dinner with her that I wanted so badly—and she did, too, I'm
sure, though she just hadn't realized it yet. No chance to recover.

At least not now.

Like a runaway train, we were moving fast down Sawtalo
Sar toward Chichal, a remote village at the base of the mountain in the Korangal Valley. Within military circles, the valley
would become famous two years later when Staff Sgt. Salvatore

Giunta would save the lives of a number of his ambushed squad to become the first living person since the Vietnam War to receive the US military's highest decoration for valor, the Medal of Honor. American troops would nickname it "The Valley of Death." We were heading down to investigate the carnage that our Air Force's bombs had created the previous day.

The sun was beginning to creep out of its hiding place, from the other side of the earth. The humidity was steadily climbing. The sun was bathing the ground, causing streams of fog to rise above the mountain floor. After the previous day's downpour, it was refreshing to feel that sun on my skin. For a moment, I would just take it in as I slid down a steep, rocky portion of the trail—on my ass. It wasn't particularly pleasant. While the rock looked fairly smooth as it glistened in the sun, it was actually more like 80-grit sandpaper. I had to use my feet to get my pants to slide down the mountain. After struggling down a small patch of rock, we came to a brief stop.

I was parched.

"Sal, you have any water left—you know, the stuff you drink?"

Sal shook his head from side to side.

"No, but I do have some of *this*." And like Derek Zoolander from the 2001 film comedy, he turned toward me with an emphasis on his crotch with his hand in the shape of a knife edge pointing to a gaping hole in his pants. And I was horrified at what I saw. It was a peep show that featured Woody Wood-pecker and his friends.

"Damn it, Sal. What the hell? Keep your boys in your pants."

I'd been trained to be prepared for the unexpected—but *this*? This was not one of those things.

"Sal, you are an ass. How in the hell did you do that?"

"Well, first my mom and dad—"

I quickly interjected to put a stop to his quick-witted answer.

"I don't need to know how babies are made Sal, but thanks."

The average person might shake their head at such immaturity. And don't even get me going on Ranger farts, which represented carpet-bombing of a different kind. OK, so this wasn't the stuff of high comedy. But I'd argue that a little harmless humor was necessary to get us through the experience. Remember, while each man here was putting his life on the line for the folks back home—that in itself requires a touch of maturity, doesn't it?—most of us were also twenty-something "kids" who'd been yucking it up like this with our pals back home only a few short years ago. And suddenly we were in a life-or-death situation, worn to the bone, and desperate for anything to keep us going. The night before, that "something" had been a fire; I'm convinced it saved our lives. Last night it had been a rainstorm that nearly killed us. This morning it was middle-school humor. In war, the whatever-works technique takes on a heightened importance.

The flip sides to such off-the-wall-ness were the quiet virtues that these same men—and those I'd trained with—had taught me: Too often, civilians only connect soldiers with combat, violence, death, and destruction. I looked at these men and thought of courage, honor, selflessness, and loyalty. I saw men who, when they signed on that dotted line to join, were in essence writing out a check for the amount up to, and including, *their lives* for the good of their country. I knew it at the time, and I know it now: *I am a better human being because I served with these men.*

Even if our humor did lean to the juvenile side.

COMING DOWN THE SIDE OF THIS GIANT MOUNTAIN WAS magical. And, no, not because of Sal's antics. I could see for miles upon miles. In fact, I could see beyond ten times the maximum effective distance of my weapon. It offered a feeling of safety knowing that I was above everything and I could see just about everything below me. It was as if I had a unique power over the valley below. For the first time since this all started, I had some control over the situation. Some control of what lay ahead of me. Control of the next step, the mission, the war. Despite being completely exhausted and without food or water, my morale was high. And, though I didn't know it at the time, it was about to get higher.

We stopped for a short security halt. People were drinking water, resting, passing off heavy items, and getting ready for what we would find in the village below. It was "all-hands-on-deck."

"Three Charlie is chasing some intel on a possible SEAL in a village," Lucas told me. His voice was etched with excitement.

"Wow, where are they?"

"On the other side of that ridgeline."

I wanted to run to the top of the ridge to join them.

"Lt. English and Three Charlie are going into a village shortly to extract him. We'll continue on to the JDAM."

We were on the verge of perhaps finding a missing Navy SEAL and confirming the death of an ACM fighter who had recently murdered sixteen men aboard *Turbine 33*. I liked how things were shaping up.

I didn't like the idea that civilians had almost certainly died in our missile strike. War is never simple. Never easy. Never just the Good Guys and the Bad Guys. As much as we want to take the fight to the enemy and allow civilians to go about their daily lives, that isn't reality. Even if I don't want to talk about it, the fact is that bad things happen to good people—innocent people—in war.

It happens in countries all over the world. In cities. In neighborhoods where children play and dogs run free. It happened on 9/11, in America. It happened in World War II: more than half of the seventy-five million people who died in that war were civilians: forty *million*. More than 100,000 civilians have died amid fighting in Afghanistan and Iraq.

I wish it were not true. But the fact that it *is* true doesn't mean the blame should be shouldered by those who seek to restore freedom and accountability to the world. People like us. We're just trying to clean up the mess that others have created—and will perpetuate if they aren't stopped.

WHEN WE ARRIVED IN THE VILLAGE, DESPITE THE LACK of gunfire, the atmosphere was tense. We knew that the JDAM bomb drops from the day prior had hit here. But given the condition of the buildings, or should I say mud huts, the remnants of a bomb being dropped were not obvious. This was a small, remote village on the side of a giant mountain. No roads, no cars, just huts and a few walking paths. One small stream. Each hut was small, no bigger than the size of an RV, and most had some type of livestock inside. It was not much different from what most would think of if I said it were similar to a historic Native American village. Very simple. No concrete, no structures other than the mud huts. Maybe ten to twenty buildings scattered on the hillside.

When we saw a little old lady and then some kids playing, they ignored us. They may have been scared, or they'd been warned by the Taliban not to engage us, or maybe they'd seen so many American soldiers over the years they were tired of us.

"Send up the Terp," I heard from the front of our formation. An interpreter is necessary to interact with the locals. The bad news, the Terp was still at the crash site with the remainder of our platoon. "The village elder is up there." When it came to language, the already-confused cultural connections between "us"' and "them" got even more confusing. Pashtun, Dari, Wazari—who knew what these folks might be speaking?

Our platoon leader, Lieutenant Howell, and Company Commander Work moved toward the front of the formation to meet a man with a "red beard." We were staggered on a small walking trail just to the northeast of the village. One man every ten to twenty feet on the opposite side of this trail, on a knee. Despite the taut-rope tension in the air, it was quiet in the village beyond.

Work, Howell, and village elder talked for agonizingly long minutes, their conversation looking as if it was getting heated. We wanted to know where the bombs had hit; he didn't seem to know. Captain Work was pointing off in the distance and raising his voice, followed by the same thing from the elder. I wish I knew what they were saying, but the speed at which they were speaking, and the thick accents, made it impossible for me to understand any of it. This, despite my "advanced" Rosetta Stone training that I completed back at Fort Lewis. I didn't know much beyond some basic greetings, how to ask for a toilet, and how to ask for fellow Americans.

Whenever our men were in a village, things got tense. Where our troops congregated, the Taliban's eyes focused and trigger-fingers started itching. For them, it was more efficient to attack a bundle then individuals here and there. And if a firefight did start, you can bet that the locals almost always blamed us for instigating it.

It made for a serious Catch-22. We couldn't afford to be fighting both the Taliban and civilians, even if it was often hard to tell the difference between the two. We needed civilians on our side. But the Taliban used them as pawns. When on their radios, for example, they would often make sure children were around them; less chance that the Americans, who had a conscience, would open fire. In the 1980s, the Soviets treated civilians with total disrespect and it boomeranged big time; a civilian uprising ultimately drove out the invaders. (Not that civilians came out of the war smiling; most had wound up in refugee camps in Pakistan and Iran.)

"Hey, Todd, think I would look good with a Crayola beard like that?" I asked our serious-faced machine gunner.

"Shut up. Sure, you'd look great. Now, pull security."

With a grin on my face, I continued doing exactly that, although it seemed to be a waste of time. The area was mostly open space. You could see for miles upon miles. The ridgeline to our front was significant, but empty. A few buildings were scattered in the distance, but mostly what I could see was mountains. Uninhabited and beautiful terrain.

I reminded myself: Forget the beauty. Look for confirmation that we'd killed someone who had just a few days earlier killed sixteen Americans with one rocket-propelled grenade. Seeing that guy dead was the beauty that I really wanted to see.

Revenge is a real emotion—and war ramps it up to the size of King Kong. I think every American felt some sense of comfort when they learned of the beginnings of the war in Afghanistan. It was a war that, initially, had lots of support. Though this would change, a November 2001 Gallup poll showed that eight out of ten Americans supported a ground war in Afghanistan.

I have to believe that support was fueled, at least in part, by the need for revenge. I felt that at the University of Arizona as soon as I heard of the attack. And I still felt it now. For me, that feeling of revenge almost spilled into hate. Hate for this place. The culture and even the people. It was borderline dangerous. A very few people planned and carried out the attack on America. But it was hard not to lump everyone into the "enemy" category.

Looking back on it, I was immature, and was fueled by the emotion of the moment.

The village elder led us back up the hillside. We rounded one corner and came upon two small livestock shelters. As we passed by, we all had eyes on it. Even though we visually cleared the shelter by peeking inside, we didn't clear every building. We trusted this elder to not lead us astray. We needed to confirm that this guy, Ahmad Shah, was in the building to which we were being led.

We walked through an open field that apparently had been recently tilled. It was covered in rocks and balls of dirt. Every few steps we'd stumble in the loose dirt. As I was trying to pull security to our flanks, I was constantly tripping and stumbling. The elder, standing off to the side, just kept pointing.

Something wasn't right. And about fifty meters into this "field" we realized what it was. This wasn't a farmer's field. It was the remnants of a building. It was *our* site. Our flattened site. The place the Air Force bombs had pummeled. Nothing was left. And when I say nothing, I mean nothing other than chunks of earth. At least that's what I thought on our first pass.

We were ordered to stop. My throat was as dry as desert sand.

"Todd, you have any water?"

"No. Been out for a while."

Frankly, he didn't look good. Not like the ox that I was accustomed to. He looked like a zombie who could fall asleep at any moment.

Our medic, Eddy, came around.

"Brooks, you good?"

I nodded.

"You good, bro?"

I nodded again. Then I got real with myself.

"Got any water?" I all but whispered.

"No, mutha fucka," he replied with gusto. He was also completely out. And so were most of the guys.

He was a loving medic and you had to know him to know that his use of the English language was a measure of endearment for his guys. The guy had a sixth sense about who needed assistance. He knew most soldiers—Todd among them—were too proud to ask for help. Within minutes Eddy had Todd hooked to an IV.

As Doc ran around rehydrating a few of the guys, we were in awe of the nothingness of this "building." *Gone. Poof.*

"They want us to completely SSE this site," said Sgt. Lucas. To search—with our bare hands—the entire field of rubble and prove that we killed their guy.

I heard Captain Work talking with Lt. Howell and SFC Congdon. After a heated discussion, they agreed that it wasn't possible to manually "process" the site with our bare hands in search of body parts of Ahmad Shah. It would require heavy machinery and a few days of work. It was like they wanted us to pull a rabbit out of a hat, but the hat was so blown to smithereens we had nowhere to even start.

Never mind what we thought. The leadership back at Bagram wanted the body of Ahmad Shah. *Now.* But we couldn't begin to find it. These leaders didn't mince their words when they called back to headquarters. A few f-bombs spiced the exchange.

The bottom line was that we didn't have the manpower or equipment to search the JDAM site properly. After the radio conversation, we agreed to do a walk-through and quick scan of the site to see if we could see any evidence. Any evidence that we had hit our target. It wasn't twenty seconds into the search when Sergeant Jones grabbed a stick and started poking at the earth.

"Holy shit, check this out!"

All of us stopped what we were doing and scurried over to see what Jones was poking at. I slung my rifle on my back in order to help him out. As I moved closer, I, too, saw it.

"What the fuck?"

It was a hand. A small hand, obviously that of a younger person. Jones was moving it around with a stick. As I processed what I was seeing, Jones reached down and flipped it out of the rubble.

Inside, I recoiled in horror. We wanted to find the body of an adult killer, not the hand of an innocent teenager. As much as I'd hoped that it was a combatant, I had trouble fathoming that a young kid would have been a real threat to us. I don't think that hand could properly grip an AK, let alone be effective against a platoon of Rangers.

My heart and mind were lost in the sight of this little hand. As much as I loved the thought of war and loved fighting for my country, this tore me apart. In my worst visions of war, I never imagined having to witness actual collateral damage. You see the word in print—"collateral damage"—and it's so damn antiseptic. So clean and neat. So unemotional.

You see a kid's hand and it's not that way at all. That hand belonged to someone's son or daughter, someone's sister or brother, someone's grandchild. Moments before those bombs hit, that child might have been kicking a soccer ball or playing tag or planning some mischief—the kind of stuff I was doing at his age. ("Mom, can I get a knife so I can make a spear?")

I felt terrible, then remembered: *In war, you don't get to feel that way.* After all, we were still out in hostile territory—in the Valley of Death. We didn't know what was coming next.

That's why soldiers spoke in code. We would say things that weren't necessarily our true feelings, but more of a cover. We spoke in code to hide our true feelings. Like the whole "mutha fucka" routine with the water. Soldiers can't just say: "I'm dying of thirst" and "OK, fine, here's some water." There is a certain machismo, a certain rawness, a certain craziness that's expected. But deep down, we can't help but *feel*.

I didn't weep or wince or grow misty-eyed after seeing that hand. But, inside, it shook me—and I don't apologize for that. Looking back, I would have been more worried if I *hadn't* felt some remorse.

Years later, Lieutenant Howell would return to this same spot and learn that we did, in fact, kill known enemy combatants in this strike. Tribal leaders told him. For now, all we had was a child's hand. Shah, we later learned, had long since fled to Pakistan and evaded us—this time.

"Let's clear this building," said Staff Sgt. Masters to his team leaders.

We wanted to search it to be sure that this neighboring building wasn't a target itself. We postured outside of the door as Sergeant Lucas prepared to breach the front. Three massive boot-kicks didn't do the job; the door bent but did not break.

"Son of a bitch," muttered Lucas.

We all chuckled a sort of nervous chuckle. Finally, Todd reared back and slammed his body through the door. It was magical. He snapped the door completely off its hinges and we all piled into the room behind him.

"Clear!" "Clear!" "Clear!"

We lowered our weapons. It was a small room, maybe twelve feet by twelve feet. In it stood only a few pieces of furniture, including a small crib. Blood-soaked bandages and used syringes lay on the ground. It looked a place where fighters had received medical care—given the crib, possibly under the veil of a child-care facility. It was obvious that Taliban fighters were being treated right here. And as always, they did so with women and children as their shield. I wasn't surprised by the trickery in the slightest. We were fighting an enemy that would go to any length to deceive us and send us home in coffins.

I was just sorry that to deal against such an enemy we'd taken the life of a child.

17

MANNA FROM HEAVEN

SITREP: 92 hours since the crash of *Turbine 33*
Chichal, Afghanistan

PLANES, WE LEARNED, WERE GOING TO BE PARACHUTING
resupplies to us. When we were told that we were finally going to
get water, food, and a few other commodities, the high-fives flew
like we'd won some sort of national football championship. Our
eyes scanned the sky for our "hope from on high."

Meanwhile, as we awaited the replenishments, I realized
something. I had trained for a year, been in Afghanistan for
four months, and been on this mission for four days, but had
not fired my rifle once. Not once. I neither lamented that idea
nor reveled in it. As they say: *it is what it is.*

"Think they'll drop some pizza?" I asked Todd, yet another
reminder of how quickly I could shift from contemplation to
pepperoni.

"As much as I would like some pizza—not funny—not even a little."

Apparently, my dry, cheese-covered question didn't give him any comfort. At least, he didn't show it. Of course, I had to pile on a bit. I mean, what else can you do when faced with a situation as miserable as this?

"C'mon, Todd, you know that an MRE-inspired pizza would hit the spot."

We both just smiled and waited for the Great Pizza Delivery Guy in the Sky. Most guys wanted something worse than they wanted pizza: nicotine. When they heard that some Copenhagen was on the incoming supply drops, you'd have thought that it was Christmas and they were six-year-olds waiting for Nintendos.

Overhead, the jet engines of a large cargo plane roared as the aircraft arced overhead. We watched as a large object exited the rear ramp of the bird, then another. As the first pallet exited, it looked as if it had a tail. It screamed toward earth, nowhere near our location—and with a parachute that hadn't deployed. Bad combo: no parachute, far away.

"Son of a bitch!" someone yelled. The second pallet hadn't fared much better. This one dropped into a valley far below us.

I was completely drained. My stomach was as empty as my water supply. Our "twelve-hour mission" was supposed to have been over days before. We desperately needed food and water. But the guys in the sky weren't doing a whole lot to help us out.

Dehydration, I suspected, was getting the better of me. When I tried to stand up, I needed to plant a fist in the ground for assistance. My lower back and right leg felt as if I had been stabbed with a hot iron. What felt like electrical shocks stabbed my right foot.

We had been asked to scan the area, looking to see if the supply drop was reachable via a short patrol. The good news: the first pallet had landed only about a quarter mile below our position, not as far as we'd originally thought. The bad news: it had landed hard, like a missile. The pallet had virtually exploded, as had most of the water bottles it was carrying. We each got a couple of full bottles, which did not last long. I drained a bottle in seconds. All of us did. We didn't know when we might get more water.

I leaned over to ask my squad leader about the other pallet that we hadn't checked on.

"Sarn't Masters, is this a good time to start dipping?" I asked with my usual sarcasm.

He just stared at me with a very serious look.

"Sure, why not add some more shit to this sandwich. In fact, we should probably do some exercise."

He cracked a big smile but stayed quiet. I could see the gears turning in his head as he shifted his gaze to the ground in front of us. And suddenly got serious.

"So, Brooks, what do you think of your first mission? Not what you expected it to be like, is it?"

This experience had hit me in a different way. Right in the gut. Truth be told, I'd been humbled. I walked into this mission feeling somewhat invincible. I think we all did. As if we would all be victorious. Never for a moment did we actually believe that the enemy would gain the upper hand.

"Sarn't—it sucks," I said. "It just sucks. War isn't like I imagined it would be. Not even a little."

"War is always throwing us pitches that we've never seen," he said. "With throwing motions that are not traditional. And we are always the visitor—I hope. That's why we need to be better than the other team."

I could relate to this analogy. We were always playing an away game, against a new pitcher, in an unfamiliar stadium, sometimes while the opponent was playing a totally different *sport*. All we could do was try to be physically and mentally tougher than the other guy.

From the moment I'd first stepped into that Chinook dual rotor helicopter, it was different. It wasn't just a story or a book that I had read about. It was *now*. *I* was the story. *I* was the guy writing the story. Each move, each emotion, and each thought mattered.

And now that the heavy lifting was over—literally and figuratively—what I realized was this: I'd been able to do far more than I'd imagined. If you'd have told me I could help pack up the remains of sixteen soldiers on the side of the mountain and survive the kind of heat, cold, and rain we did, I'd have scoffed. The experience had tested my humanity like nothing I'd ever done before.

I wouldn't say that I was scared, but I certainly had a healthy fear of the unknown. Enough to keep my eyes on the horizon for potential threats. Or to constantly be looking for the next place to seek cover should I need to bring a fight to the enemy. Was it training? Yes. But what drove me forward was also a healthy dose of fear.

Though the experience in Afghanistan would be short—far shorter than when I would later see combat in Iraq—these few days, I knew, would leave me differently than they found me.

For better or worse, I would never be the same.

WE HAD PLANNED TO SEND A SMALL PATROL IN THE area to not only secure our perimeter, but to check on the second pallet and see if we could recover anything from the poorly dropped resupply. We were not hiding in the slightest sense of the word. We were the only show in town and we knew all eyes were on us from the enemy in nearby buildings. Watching us with disgust, we presumed. Which was okay, because this type of patrol is designed to bring out anyone that might want to fight. We were there to pick a fight and eliminate anyone who opposed us. Anyone who hated our way of life so much that they were willing to die in order to change it.

Let's be honest here. None of us wanted to be in the mountains of Afghanistan right then. While we put on a façade of loving war and fighting, what we really loved was the thrill of battle. The thrill of coming out on the other side with our buddies. Yes, we were here to fight for our nation. Our way of life. Our security. But most of all, we were looking out for the well-being of the guys to our right and left.

Author Stephen Ambrose said it was the same way after the landings at Normandy in World War II. What allowed the Allied troops to prevail against the odds was more than the cause of freedom, more than individual resolve, more than even patriotism. It was men who cared about each other so much they were willing to fight to their death to save *each other.*

Our enemy was no different from us, despite their hate for our free-living way of life. Our freedom to do as we please, without excessive oversight/control of our daily lives. Our freedom to deviate from what they believed to be "the way." Today, they chose to watch us patrol, but not to pick a fight with a pissed-off and battered group of Rangers.

On one of our quick take-a-knee breaks, I was scanning the valley below when I saw a huge black cat, probably a panther. It was beautiful, sunbathing magnificently in the wild—in a war zone. My sightseeing, though, was interrupted by a briskly barked order. After a few moments of being spectators, we were told to head back to our patrol base before the sun set. We were expecting a second supply drop at any moment. We waited patiently for it. Sal was one of the more excited guys because, along with food and water, he was expecting a new pair of pants.

Once again, a cargo plane roared above us in the black sky. One pallet dropped, but we were expecting two, though we didn't hear anyone on the radio acknowledging a second. All our eyes were on the sky, our night-vision monoculars helping us to spot the pallet. The wooden crates were the size of a Volkswagen Bug and nobody wanted to be blindsided by one.

Which, of course, is exactly what happened. I heard a boom and someone yell. A member of the 75th Regimental Recon element, it turned out, had been struck by one of the pallets. I thought the worst; nobody survives being slammed from the sky by a ton or two of food and water and chewing tobacco.

As we hustled toward the pallet, one guy was sitting while another was pacing in circles, muttering obscenities under his breath. Weirdly enough, I recognized his silhouette. It was Staff Sergeant Green—yes, the same Staff Sergeant Green who had punished me just a year prior at Fort Benning. He was one of my Ranger Indoctrination Program cadre. And he was one of the most feared men to walk the halls during our class. He was short in stature, akin to a bulldog. And he had a short fuse.

For now, he wasn't a happy camper. Thankfully, the pallet had hit the ground and bounced before it hit him, so he hadn't caught full impact. I was actually glad to see and hear him stomping around and cursing. That meant he was alive. He'd only suffered bruises, both physically and mentally.

That was war: unpredictable. The pallet from the sky didn't hit some average Joe like me, a guy who'd probably be dead had he been in Green's boots. It hit one of the toughest guys in the unit, so it seemingly bounced off him. And, really, what business did it have hitting anyone? Think of all that vast empty nothingness of Afghanistan where that pallet could have *not* landed while hitting a soldier.

War was forever beating insurmountable sets of odds, another of which we'd heard amid the drops from the sky: Our 3rd Platoon had apparently recovered that Navy SEAL the villagers were harboring.

And he was alive.

18

LUTTRELL, DIETZ, AND MURPHY

SITREP: July 2, 2005
Salar Ban, Afghanistan

LIEUTENANT ENGLISH WAS THE LEADER OF 3RD PLATOON of my company. Everyone knew who he was. He was the guy with the résumé. A former enlisted man who served as a combat medic in a unit that will not be named. We will just call it "The Unit." He was a walking, talking legend. You don't just mistakenly end up in The Unit while serving in the military. You need to be the best of the best, and then some, to end up there. Even if you did manage to sneak through the cracks, you wouldn't last long. And even those guys are not your average "wash out." To even be considered for The Unit, you must be a man among men.

During the training cycle leading up to this vacation to southwest Asia, Lieutenant English would walk down the halls quietly and without drawing attention to himself—or so he thought. All of us saw him. And the mystery of him made him bigger than even the physical presence that he was. There were others I knew who had achieved legendary status, among them my former platoon sergeant, Sergeant First Class Congdon, and my former company commander, Captain Work. But English did something on July 2, 2005, that I will never forget.

Not only did he make a bold move, he made a move that many men would not have dared. After getting radio guidance that a local Afghan villager knew where one remaining "American" was being sheltered, English and his 3rd Platoon were tasked with investigating. Meanwhile, I was, as mentioned, on my way to the JDAM site with my platoon, on the opposite side of Sawtalo Sar.

English knew—and later told me in an interview—that he recognized how precious time was; he knew he needed to move his unit faster than he would have normally. Given the number of men in the unit, twenty-two, many leaders would have moved more cautiously, fearing an ambush. But English checked his risk at the door. And jumped—just like you would expect from someone with his résumé.

The men would need to move swiftly on awful terrain to the village in question, Salar Ban. Knowing the distance and the terrain, it seemed impossible. But English, the highest-ranking man in his platoon, made it to the village so fast that when I heard about it, I was stunned. His unit had gone farther than our unit in the same time frame.

"Sarn't, are we going to support Three Charlie?" I asked. *Damn, I hoped so.*

"Nope, we're going to hold strong until told to move," Masters said. "Leadership really wants this location secure."

So, we waited.

Meanwhile, Lieutenant English entered Salar Ban with a skeleton of a platoon. He decided to send forward a minimal-sized element deeper in the village to search for this missing American. As they painstakingly searched each and every crevice of the village, frustration set in when they came up empty.

"Where is the American?" one of our guys was yelling. "Where is he?"

Villagers responded with their usual blank stares. To be fair, most of them spoke or understood no English. However, when American troops are pointing rifles at you, it's amazing how well you can communicate, even if you don't know English. But these villagers were playing hard ball. They weren't friendly. Nobody spoke up.

As the squad descended the terrain, Rangers Conde, Reyes, Giunta, Glenn, Miranda, and Ski began noticing movement among a few locals. In fact, more than a few. Out of the corner of their eyes, they saw men who appeared to be hurrying in an area that they had not yet searched.

Granted, this commotion could have been an enemy getting ready to defend their village against the American invaders. And I couldn't fault them for it. Any one of those Rangers would have done the same; it just came with the territory. I greatly respected the enemy. Not their purpose or their desires, but their will to fight. Their will to defend their turf.

As the Rangers moved toward the commotion, Staff Sergeant Conde and Sergeant Reyes spotted something odd: some commotion amongst locals and a dirt-covered hand reaching out from a hole in the ground just inside one of the small structures. A large hand. A hand belonging to Petty Officer Marcus Luttrell, one of the four missing Navy SEALs who'd been ambushed about twelve hours after they'd fast-roped off a helicopter during Operation Red Wings.

"Jackpot!" we heard over the radio.

All of us knew what that meant: that despite the struggles, failures, and disappointments of the past few days, we had our guy, "The One." All of us were a bit dumbfounded that someone—hell, *anyone*—had survived a hellish ambush on that mountain. Despite my initial optimism that we would find someone alive in the beginning, I have to admit: I'd lost all hope. By now, I was only going through the motions. So, the news over the radio was like a bolt of lightning to my psyche. It jolted me back to life and reminded me why we were on this mountain.

English's ability to get his men to Salar Ban so fast may well have saved Luttrell's life; it was only a matter of time before the Taliban would have offered a villager enough money—or threatened some man's family so egregiously—that someone would have ratted on him. Had someone not rescued him, this story likely would have a much different ending—not the upbeat one we got following the gloom of sixteen deaths.

"Holy shit, can you believe it?" I said to Sergeant Jones.

"Yeah, pretty crazy. I guess he looks to be beat up, but ambulatory, so that's good."

After Reyes and Conde pulled Marcus from the small space where he'd been sheltered, they helped him back to the remainder of the Ranger platoon. Doc Ledoux and Lieutenant English were the first to greet him, along with a Special Forces medic.

"Are you okay?" English asked Luttrell, who stood 6'5". "Who are you? What is your name?"

"Marcus, ehhh . . . uggghhh . . . Luttrell. Who are you and how many men do you have?"

English looked directly into the eyes of this physically and emotionally battered man. He instinctively knew he was, indeed, an American and not a light-skinned Afghan with a Texas accent.

However, English, being a seasoned war fighter, found the question suspicious and wondered if someone—not Marcus—was inquiring. English wasn't going to bite—at least not yet.

"What's your Social Security number?"

Marcus replied with his full Social Security number, which had been scribbled into Lieutenant English's notebook for radio verification with command. The numbers matched. We had officially found one of the four recon and surveillance SEALs.

"How many men did you bring?" Marcus asked.

English finished a radio transmission that confirmed "Jackpot," then turned back to Marcus. "Enough. We have enough men. Where are your teammates?"

"Dead. They're dead. All of—"

English would interrupt Marcus, "OK, Marcus, I need you to be 100% certain. What you say from this point forward will dictate how we proceed. It will change the entire mission."

"Dead. They're all dead."

He paused, apparently, overcome by emotion—at least momentarily.

"I hope you have a lot of men," said Luttrell. "They're everywhere. All up in those mountains. How many men do you have?"

English noticed that Marcus seemingly had slowed down, possibly because the last ounce of adrenaline had drained away. Doc Ledoux was examining Marcus as this conversation continued. While Marcus was ambulatory and able to walk under his own power, and with what appeared to be all of his equipment, he was pretty beat up. The average human would probably not have been walking; hell, might not have been alive. But Luttrell wasn't your average American.

English opened his satellite imagery. He had nineteen men of Three Charlie, nine Special Forces personnel, and three Afghan special forces. Not that he told anyone.

"Marcus, can you show me where you were ambushed? Where your guys are?"

Marcus quickly pointed to a spot on the satellite imagery. Seemingly adjacent to the path that the 3rd Platoon had just walked in on. Then he circled a bigger area. And moved his finger to a slightly different spot, then another.

"Right here. They were everywhere. I hope you have a lot of guys."

"Thanks, Marcus. Now let the medics take care of you. We're gonna get you home."

"You know I'm never gonna hear the end of being rescued by you guys," Marcus said with his ever-competitive nature. The enemy had inflicted pain on Luttrell but hadn't done a damn thing to dilute his fight. No SEAL would want it known that he was rescued by a Ranger, but you can bet, deep down, he was happy to see anyone in an American military uniform.

English hustled to his platoon to brief them on the next course of action: to find the bodies of Marcus's three teammates. The mission was now recovery from here on out. No one else was alive. Thus far, we had recovered seventeen of the twenty men who'd been unaccounted for. The last three were deceased, according to Marcus—and no one had any reason to doubt him. As beat up as he was, he wouldn't have said what he did unless he was certain.

Time was now lower in priority because 3rd Platoon would be recovering bodies, not rescuing soldiers. As much as we all held out some hope, we now had some semblance of closure. Our worst fears became reality. It had clearly been a massacre, a blow that would leave us crippled for many years to come. No one, no matter how much they tell you otherwise, would ever be the same after this. The stamp of war was no different from the tattoos we get back home—they would be imprinted on us forever.

At nightfall, English had counted twenty-five men in his element: Luttrell, ten members of his platoon, the nine SF operators, the three Afghan special forces, and two Afghan locals. He designated the landing zone as XD 8045 6289—a small field where it would be easy to get the bird in and the men out as quickly as possible. As night fell—about ten hours later—Luttrell was on his way back to friendly territory.

Three Charlie now began the painstaking search for the remainder of Marcus's team. Led by SFC Fuller and the remaining members of 3rd Charlie, they combed the hills of Sawtalo Sar, specifically in the Northeast Gulch. The climb back up was back breaking, the terrain perfect for an ambush. It was no surprise why the fight had ended how it had. The mountain was a lopsided advantage to the home team.

"I think we have something," English heard from a fellow Ranger.

SFC Fuller confirmed that they'd found two men, surrounded by spent 5.56 brass: one, Danny Dietz, behind a large rock, with multiple mortal wounds and the other, Michael Murphy, in a clearing, less than a hundred feet away. Beside Murphy's body was a satellite phone he had used just a few days prior to make multiple calls for comms checks and, later, assistance. The satellite phone lay closer to Murphy, who succumbed to his injuries in an open field, likely where he had attempted to call for help back to HQ as noted in his Medal of Honor citation.

The body of Matthew Axelson would be recovered on July 10, four days after I had left the mountain. It is thought that he may have survived and evaded for a period of time longer than originally reported. In other words, he might have continued to fight after being struck by an RPG, and expended a couple more magazines before making the ultimate sacrifice for his country. He finished valiantly and I don't think he gets enough credit for the fight he put up. These are the moments that define a person. And his final ones were beyond honorable.

WHAT HAD HAPPENED? HOW HAD THE FOUR SEALS BEEN attacked and three died? What we have learned and all but confirmed on the ground is that the Shah fighting force was likely in the 8–12 men range. Video evidence and the minimal amount of 7.62mm brass found at the scene helped the determination. But given the terrain advantage that Shah and his men had, it had to have felt like dozens of enemy fighters. Long after the incident, some questions still hadn't been answered, including why, with a radio and satellite phone, they still hadn't been able to get word to the command post about where they were and what was happening. The terrain and radio choice were the obvious answer. Another lesson learned. What Luttrell, the lone survivor, was able to tell was that they had been compromised by what at least looked like a goat herder and two teenage boys. In frantic moments, they had to decide what to do with the trio. It was common knowledge that goat herders were often used by the Taliban as spies. The wise play—the play Luttrell's gut instinct told him to make—was to shoot the three on the spot. Not because the Americans were cold-hearted killers but because to let them go was to risk—seriously risk—the civilians reporting the Americans' location to the Taliban. And almost certain death for the Americans—plus, of course, ruining a mission whose ultimate goal was protection for US citizens. Much as soldiers might wish otherwise, civilians often get caught in the crossfire of war—and, in this case, the Americans hadn't started the fight. The terrorists had—on 9/11.

But the SEAL team chose to let the goat herders go, fearing that if word reached the American media, the four of them, SEALs in general, and the entire military establishment would be castigated for the war on terror's equivalent of Vietnam's "baby killers."

It seemed likely that the goat herders immediately reported the "find" to the Taliban, which quickly mustered Shah and his men, to go after the four. The three who died were killed within a few hours of the ambush, unable to escape down the Northeast Gulch.

For whatever reason, these SEALs did not have a quick reaction force that was ready to help them out. At least, not fast enough. It took far too long to get them assistance, which was a lesson learned, the hard way. We should always have our quick reaction force ready to rock and roll when this happens again.

You could argue that the three died because, collectively, they had a conscience that wouldn't allow civilians to die. You could argue lots of things. But in the end, what mattered most to me wasn't how it had all happened, but simply that it *had* happened. That three men had died. All were—and are—heroes. They fought till the very end.

I will forever speak their names.

19

FOURTH OF JULY

SITREP: July 4, 2005
Chichal, Afghanistan

THE FOURTH OF JULY, IN MY HUMBLE OPINION, IS THE most glorious of all-American holidays. Not only because of what it stands for, but because it was my grandfather's birthday. Grandpa Edward Barbero, my mother's father. Korean War Navy veteran and one of the most admirable humans I've ever met.

Why? Because he loved people, and especially his family. I remember, at age ten, watching my six-year-old sister styling his hair as he watched his favorite TV show in a La-Z-Boy recliner. She had a spray bottle, a towel, and a comb. She gave his "Dr. Phil" hair a serious makeover with bows and knots. She pulled, jabbed, and drenched him—and he just sat there laughing.

After he was finished with the treatment, he returned to his regularly scheduled life: lots of home and yard maintenance and pounding on the treadmill. He maintained his home, property, and body until he passed away at eighty-eight. A role model in every sense of the word.

I had never imagined spending my grandfather's birthday and the Fourth of July in the mountains of Afghanistan. Nor, frankly, did I realize at the moment that it actually *was* the Fourth of July. In war, days blurred together in a hurry. But Jones seemed to know.

"We're going to put on a show on that mountain," he barked at our squad. "We're going to show them what America is all about. Just look at that ridgeline for a few minutes."

I looked. And could all but feel the impending power before it even struck. The valley was eerily quiet, almost like everyone that was remaining in it knew that something was about to happen. The sun was setting, the bright valley about to become a black hole. And we knew there were plenty of Taliban fighters on that ridgeline. Somewhere.

As I looked at that glorious Sawtalo Sar and the surrounding ridgeline, I couldn't help but think about why I was out here. Not simply because I'd been sent on this current mission. But because of something greater. I was here because of my love of country and the way of life back in the grand ol' US of A. Here for the cause of freedom.

It wasn't politics. Nope, not even a little. Though I'd guess most of our platoon leaned to the conservative side of things, we weren't an overly political crew. Back in training, had we bantered with guys who didn't fit the mold? Of course. We would joke about being lovers and not fighters. Or about wanting to preserve the environment of Afghanistan from goat shit. But never would that spill onto the battlefield. At least, not when it mattered. We were a team, a family. Regardless of our political beliefs and skin colors, our blood was red.

I think some people think politics are as deep as a person can get. That's bullshit. I had guys around me who looked at the world in different political hues than I did. But the focus of our mission forced that crap aside. Politics became irrelevant. What mattered was the mission: protecting our country, protecting our men, bringing home the heroes.

I get it: politics are a necessary evil. But if politicians from both sides of the aisle could come together with one purpose, one vision, one reason *why*, we might be able to replicate the experience that I enjoyed as a member of the most elite light infantry unit on planet earth and get some actual work done in our legislative branch—instead of always fighting each other.

"One minute," whispered Masters.

In the distance you could hear the rumble of an A-10 Warthog. If you don't know the sound, you really should look it up on YouTube. As it gets closer, the Warthog sounds as if a giant lightsaber is slicing through the air above you.

BRRRRRRRRRAAAAPPPP! The distinct sound of its GAU-8 30mm cannon ripped along the ridgeline, igniting flashes of light that surpassed any Fourth of July show the Brooks household had ever seen. Explosions aplenty. My one-eyed night-vision monocular allowed me to see two shows at once. The green hue in my left eye and the fireworks in my right. I was nearly paralyzed by the sounds and visuals in front of me. It felt as if the national anthem had come to life in real time.

There was, of course, method to the madness: that mountain was still teeming with the Taliban—or, shall I say, *had been* teeming with the Taliban. Nobody in that vicinity was getting out alive after this goodbye.

BUUUUUZZZZZZ! BOOOOM, BOOOOM, BOOOOM, BOOOOM. THUMP, THUMP THUMP, THUMP! As an AC-130 unleashed a combination of 105mm and 30mm cannons, the sound and lights lit up the sky and rumbled the valley floor under my belly.

"Wow! This is insane!" I told Todd as he lay on his back.

"Yeah, this is incredible. Happy Fourth of July, buddy."

I could not believe my eyes, nor could I swell bigger with pride for country. I am guessing that the guys to my right and left felt the same; I could see all of them with huge ear-to-ear grins on their faces.

You might call my patriotism chauvinistic. But if you'll recall, my mother painted me as an earnest Forrest Gump. And I couldn't agree more. In this moment, my earnest chauvinism rang stronger than ever as the mountainside was rearranged in a massive "show of force."

Not that we should ever confuse *love for* country with believing we have a *perfect* country. I would certainly never claim that. With the good comes the ugly—whether it be Native Americans having been slaughtered, African and Caribbean slaves having been treated as less than human, the internment of Japanese Americans, and segregation/racism, we have some skeletons in our closet. And plenty of present-day malfunction in Washington, DC. I could write a whole book on that alone.

Someday, I may run for office and see what I can do about that. I may take my earnestness and healthy narcissism to help our country find a common *"why."* I'd be fueled by the same fire that burned inside me when I left the University of Arizona to join the Army. Only my motive wouldn't be revenge, but justice. To see an America that's fair for all. To root out this pandemic sense of selfishness. And to rally people around the idea of pursuing something beyond me-me-me.

In a sense, that political future might not be all that different from my military past: helping create a village where people routinely give to something greater than themselves.

Gun One, consisting of Sager and Torres. These guys carried more weight than a majority of the guys out on the mission. Not one complaint. This was immediately after returning to Bagram. (Courtesy of Orlando Torres)

My fire team following Operation Red Wings II. All of us were down at least 10 lbs and emotionally charred. The smell in this room was the smell of pure ammonia from muscle wasting. (Courtesy of Nick Todd)

July 3, 2005: While we were still on Sawtalo Sar, a memorial service was taking place at Bagram Airfield for the members of the 160th SOAR who were KIA. (Courtesy of the Madslashers)

20

COMING HOME

SITREP: Mid—July, 2005
Bagram Airfield, Afghanistan

AS THE ENGINE THRUMMED ON THE C-17 EN ROUTE home, I was lulled asleep, but not before feeling a deep sense of humility and thankfulness. First, because I was alive. And second, because who gets to begin their Ranger experience by playing in the Super Bowl? That's essentially what we had done: been involved in one of the most notable—if not also most gruesome—events in the war. I'd just participated in the largest rescue and recovery mission by a US military unit since the Vietnam War.

On the same token, coming home had its own challenges, some of it having to do with packing up my sixteen brother soldiers that day. In his book *Tribe*, Sebastian Junger refers to a study that found "that killing an enemy soldier, or even witnessing one getting killed, was more distressing than being wounded themselves. But the very worst experience, by far, was having a friend die. In war after war, army after army, losing a buddy is considered the most devastating thing that can possibly happen."

In a sense, I had sixteen friends die on that mountainside. And, with my buddies, we helped bring them home. I was among the lucky ones, however. I suffered only minor PTSD upon my return. Mainly I just felt old. I went back to school, this time at the University of Southern California—my father's and grandfather's alma mater—and what concerned my fellow students was so different from what concerned me. I was seriously pursuing a career. They were seriously pursing the next party—and girls they could make out with. Even though I was only five years older than some of these classmates, it felt more like fifteen or twenty. Honestly, I had more in common with my professors than my fellow students. That's not to blame them for not being as mature as I was, but I did have to laugh, at times, at how little they understood about the wider world. And what a warped view they had about what constituted a problem.

My problem was trying to sleep without thinking about sixteen soldiers whose bodies I'd had to squeeze into body bags, always wondering if their families ever recovered when they got that phone call or visit with the news. Their idea of a problem was a slow barista at Starbucks. We had virtually nothing in common. It was as if we spoke different languages, lived on different planets.

The lone connection I made at the University of Southern California was with Devon Kennard, a linebacker on the Trojans football team, who was in my Spanish class. He respected me. And I certainly respected him; he was not only a warrior on the field—he would go on to play in the NFL—he had the highest

GPA on the team and was involved in student-athlete health and wellness.

My research on PTSD suggests it is affected largely by a few things: the experience you had, the duration of that experience, and your upbringing. By far the most emotionally wrenching experience I had was that full day of going through dead soldiers' belongings, knowing any second I could trigger a Taliban-arranged booby trap. And then placing those dead soldiers in body bags and carrying them up the side of the mountain. I'd say that meets the "traumatic" category; but, then, I've read about World War II soldiers who spent more than a hundred days on the front lines—and saw much worse.

The family environment you grew up in is critical to how well you deal with war trauma, studies show. A 2007 analysis from the Institute of Medicine and the National Research Council found that "statistically, the twenty percent of people who fail to overcome trauma tend to be those who are already burdened by psychological issues, either because they inherited them or because they suffered abuse as children." Obviously, it isn't that simple. However, we can't ignore it either.

My PTSD was minor compared to what I know others went through, and that's where the "upbringing" part comes into play. You're more susceptible to PTSD if you were brought up in an abusive, chaotic, or dysfunctional family, all the more if your family qualified in all three categories. I was fortunate. I had a stable family life. I had support. I had modeling to fall back on. People I know say I had a good sense of "who I was" when I left, and a good sense of the same when I came home.

But few soldiers come home from war completely unscathed. I wonder if part of the problem isn't the experience of war but the experience of returning to a country in the throes of disunity and polarization. War bonds soldiers together in ways that should be the norm in our culture but no longer are. It's as if we were meant for connection, and the military solidifies such connection. But once home, we live in a world that's increasingly disconnected. We can have all sorts of online connections, but at the end of the day, what we really need is face-to-face connection. And that's happening less and less in our culture—a trend that started before the coronavirus forced social distancing in 2020.

Junger, who embedded with soldiers in Afghanistan, writes that today's vets "return from wars that are far safer than those their fathers and grandfathers fought, and yet far greater numbers of them wind up alienated and depressed. This is true even for people who didn't experience combat. In other words, the problem doesn't seem to be trauma on the battlefield so much as reentry into society."

In Afghanistan, there was resistance, an enemy, a force that our unit was charged with battling. And while mine was not an experience that resulted in victory, it was an experience that drew me close to the men around me. "Unit," of course, is the root word for "unity." That's what we had. We were one. It's a cliché, yes, but we were "all for one, and one for all."

Then we returned to a culture marked by individualized lifestyles where, even if it's not entirely true, seems to be "all for me, and me for myself." Or, condensed: "Every man for himself, every woman for herself." Back home, I'd be on my commute to school or work and some guy would cut me off and act as if I was the problem. I routinely met people who seemed so ungrateful for all they had, freedom foremost among them. Naturally, it was difficult for me to assimilate back—not necessarily because what I'd seen or been through over **there**, but the spirit of disunity I'd found back **here**.

And here's what fractures us even deeper: there's a sliver of people willing to lay down their lives for "the others in the village": police officers, firefighters, EMTs, doctors, nurses, and the military foremost among them. But there's a far larger portion of the population that wouldn't consider, for even a nanosecond, lifting a finger for police officers, firefighters, the military, and others.

The world will always be populated by givers and takers. But the imbalance in the US is tilting farther toward the "takers." And the military, when you consider it at its essence, is all about giving. About sacrificing to maintain our country's freedom. About standing up to the bully so he won't ram planes into your skyscrapers ever again.

It certainly didn't happen overnight but, when I was honorably discharged from the military in 2007, I noticed a deepening sense of "I'm-righteous-and-you're-not" thinking that pervades ages, political parties, regions—you name it. Meanwhile, the sense of acting for the "common good" seems as outdated as the eight-track tape. With that, I did serve two more years in the California National Guard.

That's why I've since joined particular organizations and boards—to work against that "all-for-me" attitude. I sit on the board of Hobizbo Inc., a real estate technology company looking to make the home-buying process simpler, the Redmond Rotary Foundation, and the Redmond Police Foundation because of my "strategic mind set," stuff I learned in the military. I have a desire to serve. I can see the big picture. And on such boards, I can be the glue that helps hold us together and accomplish more for the greater good.

The 75th Ranger Regiment consisted of guys from all sorts of backgrounds: Guys with rough childhoods who got in trouble with the law. Military brats. Guys who grew up dirt poor. But some of those guys now are some of the most well-rounded individuals I've ever met. They're the guy who'd give you the shirt off his back, even if it meant his being cold. They'd be there for you at 3 a.m. if you'd overdone it at a bar. And they've been there for me.

These are the types of individuals that we need for a healthy society. We need to forget the stereotype of these guys as somehow being suspicious and realize that, given a chance, they can be assets to any community of which they're part.

A qualifier: Every soldier doesn't come out of the military that way. You have your "super soldier" who makes every rank as fast as possible and is looked at as a shining example of the military. But a lot of these guys go through relationships as if life were nothing but a speed-dating endeavor. They burn bridges. They make unwise decisions. And I wouldn't want them anywhere near my wife and children. They simply can't be trusted to do the right thing if they are out of uniform. Like the guy in our unit who, oddly, used to brag about robbing banks once he got out of the military—and, turned out, did exactly that. But guys like this in the military are by far the exception, not the rule. Though being in the military isn't a guarantee of turning out altruistic and team-oriented, it certainly turns out people who can help us overcome the me-me-me-ness of our society.

Junger writes of how individualism and technology "seem to be deeply brutalizing to the human spirit." How the last time we had even a semblance of unity was after 9/11—and it went deeper than singing "God Bless America" before ball games. Murder rates dropped. Suicide rates dropped. Mass shootings temporarily stopped.

But now it's business as usual. We're lonely. We lack gratitude. We're divided, with incidents such as George Floyd's death doing more to tear us apart than bring us together as they should. We're all sorts of things that my guys and I were **not** when we went to war.

What also adds to the disconnect between soldier and civilian is what author and ethicist Austin Cadey calls a "shared public meaning" of the war. Villages once sent their soldiers to war as representatives of the community's greater good; the soldier and civilian had different responsibilities, but they had similar loyalty to the village. Now, American culture has been sliced and diced by liberals, conservatives, and the media; a friend once told me "the only time I really feel oneness with people is when we all rise for the national anthem before a game." Now, of course, even that doesn't work.

With all these barriers, it's rare for anyone of **this** ilk to talk to someone of **that** ilk without a personal attack or some form of virtue signaling. Unlike during the Vietnam era, military experience doesn't necessarily stamp you as a "baby killer." Now, I think it stamps you as a giant question mark. Most people don't know what to make of the folks who return from Iraq or Afghanistan. These civilians have little context. They have little connection. They have little concern. The end result, if not the out-and-out anger spewed at many Vietnam vets, seems to be a subtle distrust regarding us. A reluctance to engage us at any level regarding our experiences. A sense that whatever we did "over there," it doesn't really matter. And neither does our service to our country.

In that "pumpkin scene" from *The Return of the King*, one of the inferences is that the hobbits—the civilians—had no idea what went on in the "outside world" and, frankly, didn't really **want** to know. I think there's a bit of that going on in our culture today: people want their freedom but they don't really want to know what's required to maintain that freedom. It's a bit like that old hot dog joke: folks love eating the things, they just don't want to know what's inside.

BEING A RANGER IS A BIG PART OF MY IDENTITY, BUT it's not the ultimate part. I'd rather be remembered for being a great human being who was also a soldier than for being a great soldier who was also a human being. I don't say this as someone who pines for praise. I don't need, or expect, everybody I meet to be curious about my days as a Ranger. I suppose I just want a modicum of respect paid not so much to me, personally, but to military men and women in general.

We don't bite. We're your neighbor. In my case, we're your fellow Rotary member, your chiropractor, the fellow parent in the PTA. I suppose what I'm trying to say is I want to feel like I **belong**—not just as the Rotarian or chiropractor or PTA guy but as a former Ranger, as a fellow human. I want to feel as if I'm part of the village—not **despite** my military service but, in part, **because** of it.

During the coronavirus pandemic, did you hear what so many doctors and nurses were saying: signs and horn honks are fine, but if you really care about us, give us friggin' personal protective equipment so we can help some of these very sick people. Forget the expensive Blue Angel flyovers and send us equipment that might protect us or allow us to serve humanity. In other words: as the rest of the village, make even a small sacrifice of yourself to protect us—in the same way we're protecting you.

I can relate. If someone finds out I served and says, "Thank you for your service," I'm appreciative. That's meaningful to me. But I know vets who would find it even more meaningful if, say, a business owner learned you were a vet and were **more** interested, not **less** interested, in giving you a job because of it.

Or folks in a neighborhood welcomed your family **all the more** because you served your country, instead of being less likely to befriend you. Or the teachers at school thought it was just as cool to have an ex-Ranger come for career day as the father who works at Boeing.

Personally, more than a "thanks for your service," I want someone to be curious about my experience for all the right reasons (**"maybe I can learn from his experiences"**) rather than the wrong reasons (**"this guy must have a screw loose"**). I want to walk into the pub and, just once, have someone look past the giant pumpkin that's captivated everyone's attention and not necessarily buy me a beer, but, if they knew I was a Ranger, bring their beer to my table and say: "So, what's your story? I'm curious."

If they did, I wouldn't talk much about myself. (OK, maybe a little!) Instead, I'd tell them about twenty men who our unit was charged with bringing home. And how, although only one was still alive, all twenty—heroes in my book, every single one—made it. We had not won this battle. But we had honored a tradition of the military and left no man behind.

If we could care about strangers the same way I'd been taught to care about strangers on that mountainside, then, finally, nobody would be alone and we might knit back the frayed fabric of a great country that could be greater still.

EVERY NOW AND THEN, WHEN I'M WITH SOMEONE AND we're talking about our pasts, it will come up that I was an Airborne Ranger. Invariably, the person will almost spit out his beer or widen their eyes or do something else to suggest surprise. Hey, I get it; I look like the guy you'd call at the geeky computer place to fix your Mac. In fact, the person in my past who absolutely couldn't believe that I'd become an Army Ranger was a kid who'd been a peer in my technology classes in high school. I'm OK with people underestimating me, with their being surprised that I was once part of one of the most elite military units on the planet.

But remember how, in the end, Peter Parker gets the girl? As does the far quirkier Forrest Gump; he marries Jenny. And, of course, in *Return of the King*, the young soldier, Sam, marries the beautiful bartender.

Confession: I never lost my enthusiasm for The Unicorn. Soon after my return from Afghanistan, in the summer of 2006, I returned to Cowgirls Inc. and asked Heidi to dinner—for roughly the 756th time. Only this time was different. She hurriedly scribbled something on a piece of paper and glanced ever so briefly in my eyes.

"Sure, you can buy me a steak," she said. "I didn't think you would ever ask." She winked and rushed off to fill a drink order.

On the paper was her phone number.

We've been married now for ten years. And have two amazing children.

THAT'S A LOT OF TIME, TEN YEARS. AND I'M A BLESSED man. Marriage, fatherhood, my own business. So many layers of richness and responsibility have been added to my life since I came home from the Afghanistan mountain known as Sawtalo Sar. But not a day passes that I don't think of the sixteen men with whom I will forever be linked. Sixteen men who I had the small privilege to help bring home to the country and families they belong. Sixteen men who have done something I can only hope to someday do:

Die a hero.

EPILOGUE

AHMAD SHAH, THE TALIBAN LEADER WHO ESCAPED Operation Red Wings, died nearly three years later, on April 11, 2008. It was not a glorious death. Instead, it was the death of a petty criminal. He had kidnapped the son of a wealthy Afghan cement magnate in an attempt to extort money, but was discovered, and killed, by Pakistan Armed Forces.

On May 2, 2011, nearly a decade after the 9/11 attack, Osama Bin-Laden was shot and killed by US Navy SEALs inside a private residential compound in Pakistan.

In 2018, the War in Afghanistan passed the Vietnam War as the United States' longest military involvement against another country—ever. By June 2020, fewer than 9,000 American troops were left in the country, the nearly two-decade-long war costing the lives of 2,353 American soldiers. But the war lingered on.

Marcus Luttrell not only wrote a book, *Lone Survivor,* that was turned into the 2013 movie of the same name, but started The Lone Survivor Foundation. It's a nonprofit that empowers our wounded service members and their families to find health, wellness, and therapeutic aid. I will whole-heartedly support it for as long as I live.

After my 2005 stint in Afghanistan and completing Army Ranger School, my next deployment was to Ramadi, Iraq, the same place to which Marcus was deployed. We may very well have crossed paths without knowing it. The Battle of Ramadi was yet another version of Special Operations whack-a-mole. Little skirmish here, an IED there, a really bad dude over yonder—while executing nightly raids and capturing countless members of al-Qaeda Iraq (AQI).

Night after night, the Madslashers of 2nd Ranger Battalion chipped away at the AQI presence in Anbar province. Whether it was a boat insertion with Navy Special Warfare Combatant-Craft crew (SWCC), Stryker VDO (vehicle drop off), or MH-47 off-set infiltration, we were busy. Daytime farmer's-market raids, ambushes on weapons caches, and many, many nights spent on rooftops in Ramadi, Fallujah, and the surrounding villages—I was as busy in Iraq as I wasn't in Afghanistan.

After leaving the Army at the end of 2007, I joined the California National Guard. I went on to graduate from the University of Southern California with a bachelor's degree in biological sciences.

While living in Southern California, my Ranger buddy Justin "Hatty" Hatfield and I made a yearly pilgrimage to the grave of our buddy Devin Peguero-Cardenas in Chino Hills. We would stand shoulder to shoulder—hearts swelling with pride and eyes wet with tears—and offer him and his family a salute of respect.

Heidi and I were married May 15th, 2010, in Redding, California. And, yep, Hatty was a groomsman.

In 2014, I graduated from the Doctor of Chiropractic program at the University of Western States in Portland.

The very same year we welcomed our first child, Ryle, pronounced like Kyle but with an "R." In a serendipitous turn of events, Heidi found out she was pregnant with him on June 28, 2013, eight years to the day I suited up for recovery of *Turbine 33* on Sawtalo Sar.

Heidi and I started a chiropractic clinic in Redmond, Washington, and settled in nearby Everett. In 2017, we added a daughter, Evynn, to the family. It was "home delivery" at its best—and most awkward. Though this wasn't completely the plan, I assisted with the delivery, the event being perfect in all its imperfection.

Meanwhile, I've found ways to repurpose the same spirit that led me to become a Ranger. I did so by realizing what really floated my emotional boat was simply helping other people. Taking away their pain, helping them optimize their health. And teaching others to do the same. A great friend, marketing strategist, and mentor, the "Dark Lord," Marc Swerdlick, taught me that you can either do what you love for a living or do whatever allows you to amass the resources to do what you love. It doesn't matter. Either way, do what you love. And I do.

In a similar way, I was able to transfer the shared vision I had with my buddies in Afghanistan and Iraq to the friends I have in Rotary: in both cases, we had—and have—a shared vision, a shared love for country, and a shared affection for fellow human beings.

Hatfield, my Ranger buddy, once told an interviewer: "Brooks always had a plan in place, whether he knew it or not. He saw the endgame, the bigger picture." I like that. It's true. I am always thinking big. Even if the idea is sometimes bigger than my britches.

The military taught me a lot about people. And as much as I was cool to the idea of Rangers having to be pals with the locals in Afghanistan, that spirit of bridge-building has carried over to my life in America. I have patients of all different kinds of ethnic, political, cultural, and regional backgrounds; it's a huge advantage—and, frankly, something I do fairly well—to appreciate all of them for the unique people they are. For my buddy who likened me to Peter Parker in *Spider-Man*, I suppose if I have any superpower it's the ability to sit in a room of environmentalists one day and NRA proponents the next—and enjoy them both. I am, a friend once said, "an extroverted introvert."

Finally, remember the ring the Rangers found at the *Turbine 33* crash site? In 2019, nearly fourteen years after that event, I connected with the widow of Major Stephen Reich, whose ring was found in the ashes. Jill Blue Reich sent a couple of beautiful pictures of his band on her finger. For some reason, that comforted me to no end, as did the realization that, in true Night Stalker spirit, she has remained strong and taken life by the horns.

A photo that Jill Blue Reich, widow of Major Stephen C. Reich, sent to me when I asked if she ever received "the ring." (Courtesy of Jill Blue Reich)

Delong, myself, Peters, and Hatfield after our first deployment as Rangers. We were about to hit the Seattle bar scene and Cowgirls Inc. so that I could ask The Unicorn out on a date. (Courtesy of Tory Brooks)

After returning from Iraq in 2007, The Unicorn and me on a Caribbean cruise. (Courtesy of Tony Brooks)

ACKNOWLEDGMENTS

WITH SO MANY PEOPLE TO THANK FOR MAKING THIS possible, I want to be clear—it took a village.

To Heidi (The Unicorn), Ryle, and Evynn, thank you for giving me the strength to see the big picture. It was, and always will be, you that drove this race car across the finish line. You've made my life worth living beyond just day to day, given me a purpose to live and serve. A reason to leave the world better than I found it. I'm confident you will go out and change the world for the better. And don't be afraid to tell **your** stories. I love you all.

To my family, Kathleen (Mom), Stephen (Dad), Michael, and Kristina, I love you. Thank you all for always being there when I needed you and for supporting me along the way.

To all of my extended family, including those with whom I have lost touch, thank you for being a part of my life and supporting me along my journey.

Justin "Hatty" Hatfield, Rick English (passed from cancer on 9/1/2014 and is survived by his wife Zhara Zwelling- English), Orlando Torres, Felipe Peters, Cpt. Eric Delong, Jeremiah Congdon, Sam Crino, Peter Fortier, John Larson, Christopher Masters, Lt. Col. Jimmy Howell, Brigadier General Pat Work, Austin Roberts, Ray Fuller, Tony Rangel, Nick Todd, Nick Moore, Mario Reyes, Jason Conde, Paul Bruss, Jill Blue Reich, Vincent "Rocco" Vargas, Jamie Spence, Mike Jones, Toby Halbert, Tom Sager. I appreciate all of you for your contributions.

ACKNOWLEDGMENTS

Greg Johnson and the staff at Wordserve Literary: thank you for believing in me and my story.

Ed Darack, Jeff Layton, and Robin Ryan: thank you for your mentorship along the way.

Justice (ret.) Anthony Kennedy: I appreciated your cheer-leading—long before I landed a publisher.

Diversion Books, publisher Scott Waxman, and editor in chief Keith Wallman, thank you for this opportunity to share my story with the world. I look forward to many more to come.

All of the Rangers whom I had the pleasure of serving with, learning from, and being inspired by, thank you! Like the sixteen on board *Turbine 33*, you'll never be forgotten.

INDEX

INDEX

INDEX

INDEX

ABOUT THE AUTHORS

DR. TONY BROOKS IS A FORMER MEMBER OF 1ST Platoon, Charlie Company, 2nd Battalion of the 75th Ranger Regiment. He deployed to Afghanistan (2005) and Iraq (2006 & 2007), graduated from Ranger School in class 04–05. Brooks also served in the California National Guard from 2008–2010.

He has been featured in *Backbone*, a documentary on chiropractic and the military; was featured on the Science Channel's *Black Files Declassified*; and appeared in Smithsonian *Air and Space* magazine regarding Operation Red Wings.

He is a sought-after keynote speaker, owns and operates Structural Chiropractic in Redmond, Washington, and serves on the board of Hobizbo Inc. He founded Objective Health, a health food and supplement brand, to improve the health of veterans and their families. Brooks is a past president of the Redmond Rotary Club, and serves on Redmond Rotary's Foundation board as well as volunteers on the Redmond Police Foundation. *Leave No Man Behind* is his first book.

He lives in Everett, Washington, with his wife, Heidi, and two children, Ryle and Evynn.

Contact author Dr. Tony Brooks at www.drtonybrooks.com.

ABOUT THE AUTHORS

BOB WELCH IS THE AUTHOR OF MORE THAN TWENTY-FIVE books, including half a dozen related to war. His book about the first nurse to die after the Normandy landings in World War II, *American Nightingale,* was featured on ABC's *Good Morning America* and was an Oregon Book Award finalist. His book, *The Wizard of Foz: Dick Fosbury's One-Man High-Jump Revolution,* was named the 2019 Book of the Year by the Track & Field Writers of America.

He lives in Eugene, Oregon, with his wife, Sally.